The Marriage Communication Toolkit

How to Talk and Truly Be Heard

Daniel Moore

Connecting the Gap Ministries

First published by Connecting the Gap Ministries 2026

First Edition

ISBN: 979-8-234-01500-6

Visit the author's website at www.connectingthegap.net or www.marriagelifeandmore.com.

To my wife, Michelle,

You are the steady place in my life when everything else moves.

Your strength carries us, your resilience inspires me, and your love changes me daily.

Thank you for loving me with patience when I'm hard to love, with grace when I don't deserve it, and with a faithfulness that reminds me what God's love looks like in human form.

This book exists because you exist in my life.

I love you — always.

Daniel

Contents

Preface

We didn't originally set out to write a book about communication.

We set out to help marriages.

As we have been walking alongside couples in marriage ministry, listening to stories, praying through tears, and celebrating reconciliation, one pattern became unmistakably clear: most marriages are not destroyed by a lack of love, they are slowly weakened by a lack of understanding.

Husbands and wives sit in the same room, share the same home, attend the same church, raise the same children... yet feel miles apart. Conversations turn into arguments. Silence replaces connection. Good intentions become hurt feelings. And eventually, two people who genuinely care for each other begin to feel unheard, unseen, and misunderstood.

Again and again we heard the same words: *"We just can't communicate."*

Not *"we don't love each other."* Not *"we don't want this marriage."* But *"we don't know how to talk to each other anymore."*

That is not an accident.

God created marriage with purpose, order, and design. He did not leave something this important up to human instinct or personality. Scripture gives us a clear blueprint for how men and women are wired, how they process, how they respond, and how they are meant to speak and listen to one another. When His design is followed, communication produces unity, safety, and intimacy. When it is ignored, confusion and division naturally follow.

And the enemy knows this.

Satan cannot create — he can only distort. If he can twist communication, he can weaken connection. If he can weaken connection, he can harden hearts. And if he can harden hearts, he can slowly divide what God joined together. Many couples assume their conflict is about finances, parenting, expectations, or personality differences, when in reality those are only the surface. Underneath is a breakdown in understanding, hearing words but missing meaning, reacting to tone instead of heart, defending instead of receiving.

In other words, two people talking... but neither truly being heard.

This book was born out of a burden and a hope.

The burden is seeing sincere believers struggle in their marriages not because they lack faith, but because they lack tools. Many couples love God and love each other, yet they unknowingly communicate in ways that create distance instead of unity. They pray together but still fight. They want peace but repeat the same conversations with the same painful results.

The hope is that God has already provided answers.

His Word does not only tell us *what* marriage should be — it teaches us *how* to live it. Within His design are practical, understandable principles that change the way husbands and wives listen, respond, express emotion, resolve tension, and pursue connection. Communication, when done God's way, is not about winning arguments. It is about understanding hearts.

The goal of this book is not merely to improve conversations but to restore connection.

You will find truths from Scripture paired with practical techniques you can apply immediately. Some may challenge habits you've carried for years. Some may explain reactions you never understood, in yourself or your spouse. Others may feel surprisingly simple yet powerfully freeing. The aim is not perfection, but clarity. Not performance, but unity.

My prayer is that as you walk through these pages, you will begin to recognize patterns that once caused frustration and replace them with understanding. That defensiveness will give way to patience. That assumptions will give way to curiosity. And that conversations which once ended in hurt will begin to produce peace.

Most of all, I pray your marriage becomes a place where both of you can once again speak... and truly be heard.

When communication reflects God's design, it doesn't just solve arguments, it strengthens covenant.

And that is what this book is really about.

Acknowledgements

To God

All glory belongs to You, the One who created and sustains marriage. Every truth in these pages flows from Your Word and Your grace. May You use this book to draw hearts closer to You and to one another.

To my wife, Michelle

Thank you for walking beside me in every season, in marriage, ministry, and life. Your faith steadies me, your love humbles me, and your commitment reminds me daily what Christ-centered love looks like.

To our children, their spouses, and our grandchildren

You are one of God's greatest blessings in our lives. My prayer is that you see not perfect examples, but faithful ones, people learning to trust Jesus and love well, one day at a time.

To the listeners of Marriage Life and More and Connecting the Gap Podcasts

Thank you for letting me speak into your lives and for speaking into mine. Your encouragement and testimonies continually remind me why this message matters.

To you

I'm grateful you picked up this book. May it guide you closer to Christ and help your relationships reflect His design and His heart.

God's Blueprint for Communication in Marriage

Biblical Foundation: Genesis 2:24, Proverbs 18:21, Ephesians 4:29

In the cozy living room of their suburban home, Sarah stood by the window, her arms crossed tightly against her chest. The glow of the evening sun streamed through the glass, casting warm hues over the plush furniture, but inside her, a storm was brewing. Her husband, Mark, was sitting on the couch, fiddling with the remote, seemingly oblivious to the tension in the air.

"Mark, can we talk?" Sarah finally said, her voice a mix of hope and frustration.

"About what?" he replied without looking up, his eyes glued to the television screen.

Sarah took a deep breath, trying to muster the courage to voice her worries. "About the party this weekend. I need to know if you're going to help with the preparations or if I'm doing it all alone again."

Mark's eyebrows furrowed in irritation. "I thought we agreed that I would handle the drinks and music. Isn't that enough? You always want to micromanage everything!"

The words stung. Sarah felt a surge of frustration. "Micromanage? I want to make sure everything goes smoothly! You never seem to take these things seriously."

"Seriously? You're making it sound like I don't care. I do care! I thought we could have some fun and keep it casual. Why do you have to make everything so stressful?"

As the exchange escalated, the misunderstanding deepened. What Sarah saw as Mark's lack of commitment, he perceived as her need to control every detail. Both spoke from their hearts but listened only to their frustrations.

"I'm not trying to control everything, Mark! I just want us to be on the same page," she exclaimed, her voice rising.

"And I just want you to trust me to handle my part!" he shot back, finally setting the remote down, frustration written all over his face.

The room fell silent, the air thick with unresolved tension. Both felt hurt and misunderstood, standing on opposite sides of an emotional divide that seemed to widen with every word. What began as a simple conversation spiraled into a bitter argument, leaving both upset and alone in their respective corners of the room. Each of them hoped for understanding, yet found only walls built higher by miscommunication.

As the sun dipped lower into the horizon, shadows crept across the floor, mirroring the growing distance between them, a couple who loved each other, yet struggled to find the words to bridge the gap.

This scenario, a couple caught in a cycle of defensiveness and misunderstanding, is increasingly common in today's society and reflects deeper issues many marriages face. Statistics reveal a troubling trend: the rate of divorce in the United States hovers around 40-50% for first marriages,

with subsequent marriages having even higher rates of dissolution. According to a study by the National Center for Family and Marriage Research, communication problems are cited as a leading cause of divorce, with 65% of participants identifying it as a significant factor.

This pattern is not confined to a specific demographic or faith group; it extends into Christian communities as well. Research conducted by the Barna Group indicates that among practicing Christians, frequent miscommunication also contributes to marital dissatisfaction. Their findings show that many couples report not engaging in meaningful conversations about their feelings, desires, or struggles, leading to a façade of harmony that masks underlying discord. In fact, a survey from Lifeway Research found that more than half of churchgoers with spouses believe their marriage requires more intentional effort in communication.

The consequences of poor communication are staggering, beyond simply resolving conflicts, they can erode the very foundation of relationships. Misunderstandings often lead to what can be described as "hateful miscommunication," where the words spoken are laden with frustration and resentment. Studies suggest that couples who engage in destructive arguing patterns, such as name-calling, blaming, and stonewalling, are often trapped in cycles that exacerbate their issues. The American Psychological Association notes that such negative interactions create a corrosive environment, fraught with emotional distance and increasing discontent, which ultimately can lead to breakdowns in intimacy and trust.

Furthermore, the cultural shift towards individualism and the prioritization of personal fulfillment can compound the problem. With growing expectations that partners meet all emotional needs, many individuals become frustrated when their spouse fails to communicate effectively or to understand their concerns naturally. A lack of conflict resolution skills can trigger a downward spiral in which couples increasingly retreat into their own corners, believing the other is unyielding or uncaring, deepening the isolation within the marriage.

As our society grapples with these issues, it becomes crucial for couples to develop healthier communication strategies. Resources such as marriage counseling, workshops, and communication-focused reading materials can be invaluable. Within the Christian context, promoting open dialogues guided by biblical principles of love, patience, and understanding may not only repair communication issues but also strengthen marriages at their core, moving them away from the statistics of failure toward stories of redemption and unity.

This book is an honest effort to equip couples with vital tools and principles that can transform communication, promoting deeper understanding and stronger connections in marriages. At its core, this book seeks to offer both Biblical wisdom and practical strategies that guide couples in navigating the complexities of marital communication. The example presented earlier reflects a common struggle where miscommunication can lead to strife and distance, making it all the more important to address these issues head-on with actionable insights rooted in Scripture.

God's design for marriage emphasizes unity and understanding. Ephesians 4:29 highlights this when it says, *"Do not let any unwholesome talk come out of your mouths, but only what is helpful for building others up according to their needs, that it may benefit those who listen."* In each chapter, we will explore how to apply such Biblical principles, focusing on creating a communication environment where partners feel valued and heard. By implementing practical communication techniques alongside these scriptural foundations, couples can learn to articulate their feelings and resolve conflicts more effectively, thus nurturing their relationship.

We will also aim to provide insight into the dynamics of listening, a crucial element often overlooked in discussions of communication. James 1:19 instructs us to be *"quick to listen, slow to speak, and slow to become angry."* This principle serves as a guiding framework throughout this book, encouraging couples to prioritize listening to understand their partner's perspective. The exercises and techniques expressed will enable couples to practice active listening, moving beyond mere hearing to genuine comprehension and empathy.

Additionally, we will address the importance of resolving conflicts in a healthy manner, drawing inspiration from Proverbs 15:1: *"A gentle answer turns away wrath, but a harsh word stirs up anger."* This scripture offers practical advice on de-escalation techniques, conflict-resolution strategies, and the practice of humility and grace in conversations. By approaching disagreements with a posture of grace and understanding, couples can cultivate an atmosphere where love and respect reign, even in times of conflict.

Overall, this book is designed to serve as a resource that not only identifies common pitfalls in marital communication but also provides real solutions based on a solid biblical foundation. Through dedicated practice and a commitment to applying these principles, couples can experience a transformation in their interactions, leading to a stronger, more resilient marriage that honors God. Our prayer is that each couple who engages with this book will find healing and growth, moving toward a deeper partnership grounded in love and understanding.

As we step into this journey together, you are taking a significant step toward strengthening the precious relationship you share with your spouse. Communication is the lifeblood of any marriage, and this book is designed to guide you through the essential principles and practical tools that can transform the way you interact with each other. Together, we will explore biblical insights and apply them in ways that not only address misunderstandings but also encourage an environment of trust and open dialogue. Whether you're facing complex challenges or simply wish to strengthen your connection, this book invites you to be intentional about growing in communication, leading to a more fulfilling and harmonious marriage, God's way. We are excited to walk alongside you and witness the positive changes that can unfold as you engage with these principles and practices.

The Purpose of Communication in God's Design for Marriage

In God's design for marriage, communication serves not only as a tool for sharing thoughts and feelings but also as a vital axis around which relational health and intimacy revolve. At the heart of this divine blueprint is the understanding that husband and wife are called to be one flesh, as stated in Genesis 2:24: *"For this reason a man will leave his father and mother and be united to his wife, and they will become one flesh."* Effective communication underpins this unity, helping couples navigate differences and deepen their bond. It allows partners to share their hearts, encourage one another, and address issues that can arise in the shared life they create together.

The importance of communication is further emphasized in Ephesians 4:15, which encourages believers to *"speak the truth in love."* This verse highlights that communication should not only be honest but also compassionate. When spouses express vulnerability and truth, they create a safe space for one another, allowing for emotional and spiritual growth. However, this requires conscious effort; it's not merely about exchanging words but engaging in heartfelt dialogues that promote understanding. Proverbs 25:11 aptly describes this, stating, *"Like apples of gold in settings of silver is a ruling rightly given."* Intentional, thoughtful communication is a precious aspect of marital life that reflects God's wisdom and encourages unity.

Conversely, when couples fail to align their communication with God's principles, the ramifications can be severe. Poor communication often leads to misunderstandings, resentments, and conflict. James 4:1-2 poignantly reminds us, *"What causes fights and quarrels among you? Don't they come from your desires that battle within you? You desire but do not have; so you kill."* A lack of effective communication can exacerbate internal conflicts, leading to hurtful words and actions that can fracture the very foundation of the marriage. In times of strife, spouses may fall into patterns of blame, anger, or withdrawal, creating an environment steeped in bitterness rather than love.

When communication is unmanaged or overlooked, issues that could be resolved through dialogue become insurmountable obstacles. As stated in Proverbs 18:19, *"A brother wronged is more unyielding than a fortified city; disputes are like the barred gates of a citadel."* This highlights how unresolved conflicts can become barriers hard to overcome, leading to emotional walls rising between partners. Miscommunication can sow seeds of mistrust and distance, leading couples to feel isolated rather than united, which is the opposite of God's intent for marriage.

Communication is the lifeblood of any marriage, designed by God to promote intimacy and unity among partners. It is essential for expressing love, resolving conflict, and maintaining relational harmony. When couples prioritize biblical principles of communication, truth, love, empathy, and humility, they not only honor God's design but also experience the rich rewards of companionship and mutual support. Conversely, neglecting these principles can lead to misunderstandings, discontent, and emotional separation. Therefore, embracing the importance of God-honoring communication is crucial for nurturing the marriage God desires for each couple.

One of the most commendable examples of effective communication in the Bible can be found in the relationship between Priscilla and Aquila. This dynamic couple, mentioned in the New Testament (Acts 18:1-3; Romans 16:3), exemplifies how mutual respect, understanding, and a commitment to open communication can create a strong partnership in both life and ministry.

Priscilla and Aquila were tentmakers by trade, sharing not just a profession but an unwavering bond as husband and wife. Their collaboration extended beyond daily work, as they actively engaged in ministry together, often hosting gatherings in their home for teaching and worship. A significant moment highlighting their communication occurs when they encounter Apollos, a learned man teaching about Jesus but lacking a complete understanding of the Gospel (Acts 18:24-26). Rather than confront him publicly or dismiss him, Priscilla and Aquila invite Apollos into their home and explain the way of God more accurately. This approach illustrates their dedication to grace-filled communication, prioritizing understanding over argument.

The attributes displayed by Priscilla and Aquila are particularly relevant for modern marriages. First, their example reinforces the necessity of mutual support in communication. They actively listened to one another and collaborated as equal partners, recognizing each other's strengths. This dynamic reflects God's design for marriage, wherein husbands and wives are called to be each other's helpers (Genesis 2:18) and to work together in harmony. In practical terms, couples can apply this by creating an environment where each partner feels heard and valued, enabling open discussions of ideas, feelings, and concerns without fear of judgment.

Additionally, their willingness to communicate truth with love is a principle that God desires in marriages today. Ephesians 4:15 guides us to *"speak the truth in love."* Priscilla and Aquila did not shy away from addressing inaccuracies in Apollos' teaching; instead, they approached the matter with kindness and respect. This highlights the importance of maintaining a tone of love and encouragement, even when addressing complicated subjects. Couples can learn from this model by ensuring their discussions prioritize empathy, build each other up, and approach challenging topics with humility rather than harshness.

Priscilla and Aquila exemplified how effective communication can strengthen a marriage and promote a shared mission. Their partnership reminds us that mutual respect, active listening, and speaking truth with love are essential components of a God-honoring marriage. As couples apply these attributes in their relationships, they can cultivate an atmosphere of understanding and support that brings them closer together in their walk with the Lord and with each other.

Understanding Emotional, Spiritual, and Verbal Connections

In a Godly marriage, the essence of a strong and lasting union lies in three critical connections: **emotional**, **spiritual**, and **verbal**. Each of these connections plays a vital role in promoting a relationship that honors God and reflects His love for humanity. Let's explore these connections deeper.

Emotional

The emotional connection in a Godly marriage is a vital thread that holds the relationship together. This connection goes beyond mere affection or attraction; it encompasses empathy, trust, vulnerability, and deep understanding between partners. Here's a closer look at this vital aspect of a marital relationship.

Understanding the Emotional Connection
1. Empathy and Understanding:

The emotional connection thrives on both partners' ability to empathize with one another, recognizing and validating each other's feelings. This requires stepping into each other's shoes, experiencing each other's joys and sorrows, and offering support during challenging times.

Romans 12:15 instructs us: *"Rejoice with those who rejoice; mourn with those who mourn."* This passage emphasizes the need for emotional solidarity within relationships.

2. Vulnerability and Openness:

Emotional intimacy can only grow in an atmosphere that encourages vulnerability. When both partners share their thoughts, fears, dreams, and insecurities openly, they build a trust that strengthens their bond. Vulnerability allows spouses to be authentic with each other, leading to deeper levels of connection.

Ecclesiastes 4:9-10 reminds us that *"two are better than one,"* emphasizing the support partners can offer one another during life's difficulties.

3. Support and Encouragement:

A strong emotional connection is marked by mutual support and encouragement. Spouses should have the ability to lift one another up during tough seasons, offer constructive feedback, and celebrate each other's successes without jealousy.

Proverbs 27:17 states, *"As iron sharpens iron, so one person sharpens another,"* calling for spouses to challenge and uplift each other in love.

Consider the story of Jake and Caroline, a married couple navigating the challenges of raising children while balancing their careers. During a particularly stressful week, Jake felt overwhelmed by work, while Caroline was dealing with her own anxieties about their children's schooling. Instead of each coping in isolation, they chose to engage in an intentional conversation that showcased their emotional connection.

Jake initiated the talk by voicing his struggles, saying, *"I've been really stressed about work lately, and it's making me irritable."* Caroline listened attentively, responding with empathy, *"I understand. I've been feeling anxious about the kids and trying to balance everything, too. It can feel like we're carrying so much."*

In that moment, acknowledgments flowed from both sides, and they shared their feelings of vulnerability. They prayed together, inviting God into their discussion for guidance and strength. This interaction not only affirmed their love for one another but also deepened their emotional connection as they realized that they were teammates in life's challenges.

Ultimately, this conversation led them to create a new routine: meeting at the end of each week to check in with each other, discuss any worries, and celebrate small victories, thereby reinforcing their emotional bond and building resilience in their relationship.

This concept can be applied in any relationship using the following steps:

1. Intentional Conversations: Regularly set aside time to discuss feelings, challenges, and aspirations.

2. Active Listening: Practice focused listening where each partner feels truly heard and understood.

3. Prayer and Support: Make prayer a priority in addressing emotional burdens, inviting God's presence into the marriage.

4. Reassurance of Love: Frequently express love and appreciation through words and actions, reinforcing the emotional safety net that each partner provides.

The emotional connection in a Godly marriage is paramount to nurturing a loving and resilient relationship. Through empathy, vulnerability, and support, partners can build a deep emotional bond that honors God and strengthens their union.

Spiritual

The spiritual connection in a Godly marriage serves as a fundamental pillar that not only supports the relationship between spouses but also anchors it in a shared commitment to God. This connection entails growing together in faith, aligning spiritual values, and cultivating a relationship that seeks to honor God in every aspect of life. Let's explore this concept in detail.

Understanding the Spiritual Connection
1. Shared Faith and Values:

The spiritual connection is primarily built on shared beliefs and principles that guide both partners' lives. A strong foundation in faith means that both individuals are not just followers of Christ individually, but also as a couple. This shared faith influences how they approach challenges, make decisions, and support one another.

2 Corinthians 6:14 states, *"Do not be unequally yoked with unbelievers,"* emphasizing the importance of sharing the same spiritual foundation for a healthy partnership.

2. Prayer and Spiritual Practices:

A thriving spiritual connection is marked by regular prayer together, Bible study, and participation in spiritual practices. These activities invite God into their relationship, facilitating a deeper bond as they grow in their understanding of His will.

Matthew 18:20 emphasizes, *"For where two or three gather in my name, there am I with them,"* highlighting the power of collective prayer and worship.

3. Mutual Encouragement in Faith:

In a Godly marriage, spouses encourage one another in their individual spiritual journeys. They celebrate each other's victories, pray for one another during struggles, and challenge each other to grow closer to God.

Hebrews 10:24-25 encourages believers to *"spur one another on toward love and good deeds"* and to *"not give up meeting together,"* both of which are essential for mutual spiritual growth.

A good example is Rob and Lacy, a couple who have been married for several years. Initially, their spiritual lives were somewhat parallel but separate; they attended church services and prayer meetings alone with friends and family. However, they recognized the importance of strengthening their spiritual connection as a couple.

One evening, as they sat together in their living room, Rob suggested they start a monthly practice of reading through a devotional book together. *"I feel like we spend so much time on our individual faith journeys, but we should also cultivate our faith as a couple,"* he expressed. Lacy wholeheartedly agreed, recognizing that they had been missing this vital aspect of their relationship.

The couple began to carve out time every Sunday evening to read the devotional aloud, engaging in discussions about what they were learning and how they could apply those lessons in their lives. They also dedicated time to praying for each other's goals, dreams, and challenges, lifting each other before the Lord.

One day, Lacy faced a challenging situation at work, feeling stressed and overwhelmed. Rob, knowing that she was struggling, lovingly reminded her of a specific verse they had read together: "Cast all your anxiety on him because he cares for you" (1 Peter 5:7). He offered to pray with her right then, demonstrating the strength of their spiritual connection.

The couple's intentional efforts to grow spiritually together not only deepened their relationship, but the increased prayer, communion in Scripture, and shared spiritual goals also fortified their individual faith. Their marriage began to reflect more of Christ's love and grace, positively impacting those around them.

Four simple steps can be taken to help build the spiritual connection in your marriage as a couple:

1. Regular Joint Prayer: Create a habit of praying together daily or weekly to bring requests and praises before God.

2. Bible Study Together: Choose devotionals or Bible studies to read and discuss together to cultivate spiritual dialogue.

3. Attend Church as a Unit: Make attending services together a priority, including Sunday worship, mid-week services, or any church-related activities.

4. Pursue Joint Ministry Opportunities: Get involved in serving opportunities or church ministries as a couple to grow together in faith and purpose.

My wife Michelle and I used to attend a church where we served separately for the majority of the time. When God led us to a different church, we decided to start serving together more often. We both still have areas where we serve individually, but there are multiple areas that she and I serve together.

In another example, I have had a Bible study podcast for over 5 years. A little over a year ago, at the time of writing this book, she joined me on the podcast to start another branch of the ministry focused on marriage. We now have a marriage ministry that we operate together as a couple, branching into the church and our own individual ministry as a couple. Our spiritual and emotional connection has grown in leaps and bounds, and we feel we are as close as ever in our joint relationship!

The spiritual connection in a Godly marriage is essential to instigating a deep, abiding relationship. Through shared faith, prayer, and spiritual encouragement, you, as a couple, can build a strong spiritual bond that not only enriches your marriage but also reflects God's love in your lives, just as Rob and Lacy, Michelle, and I did.

Verbal

The verbal connection in a Godly marriage is essential for ensuring that spouses communicate effectively and lovingly with each other. This connection encompasses the way couples speak to one another, the words they choose, and their willingness to express encouragement, love, and truth. A strong verbal connection creates understanding and intimacy in marriage and creates a safe environment for open dialogue.

Understanding the Verbal Connection
1. Effective Communication:

At the heart of the verbal connection is effective communication, which involves more than just talking; it requires active listening and responding thoughtfully. Being able to express thoughts and feelings clearly allows each partner to understand the other's perspective.

James 1:19 encourages us to *"be quick to listen, slow to speak, and slow to become angry."* This passage emphasizes the importance of listening before responding.

2. Words of Affirmation:

Using words of affirmation helps partners feel valued and loved. Compliments, appreciation, and encouragement strengthen the emotional bond, reinforcing the positive atmosphere in the relationship.

Proverbs 16:24 reminds us, *"Gracious words are a honeycomb, sweet to the soul and healing to the bones."* Words can have a powerful effect on our emotional well-being.

3. Constructive Conflict Resolution:

Disagreements and conflicts are inevitable in any relationship, but how couples handle these situations reveals the strength of their verbal connection. Healthy communication during conflict involves expressing concerns respectfully and seeking solutions together.

Ephesians 4:15 emphasizes the importance of *"speaking the truth in love,"* underscoring that honesty should always be tempered with love and kindness.

Paul and Karen are a married couple navigating the ups and downs of daily life. Early in their marriage, they realized that, while they loved each other deeply, their communication style was lacking. They often found themselves in disagreements that escalated because they did not take the time to listen carefully or express their feelings appropriately.

One particular instance during a stressful week, Paul inadvertently upset Karen by failing to acknowledge an important event she had planned for their friends. Instead of calmly discussing her feelings, Karen initially reacted with frustration, stating, "You never care about what I do!" This response led to a tense exchange in which both were quick to protect their feelings rather than to understand one another.

Recognizing the need for healthy communication, they revisited their approach. That evening, they sat down to talk and decided to use "I" statements to express themselves. Karen began, "I felt hurt when the event was overlooked because I had invested a lot of time planning it." Paul listened and then responded, "I'm really sorry I didn't consider your effort. I care about what you do, and I appreciate your hard work."

Through gentle, honest dialogue, they discussed their feelings without losing sight of their love for one another. Paul also expressed his struggles with work stress that had distracted him. This openness allowed them to support each other better and acknowledge that misunderstandings occur in any relationship.

Going forward, Paul and Karen committed to making daily check-ins a practice where they would express gratitude, discuss minor matters before they became significant, and address any concerns constructively. They even developed a ritual of sharing three things they appreciated about each other each week, which further encouraged positivity in their verbal exchanges.

Formulating good practices verbally in a marriage can be a game-changer when communication starts to escalate. Some practical steps can be taken to help strengthen the verbal bond between a couple, such as:

1. Regular Check-Ins: Establish a habit of checking in with each other regularly to discuss feelings, challenges, and affirmations.

2. Active Listening: Practice focused listening, ensuring that each partner feels heard. Repeat back what the other has said to ensure clarity.

3. Use of Affirmations: Make it a point to express appreciation for one another. Compliment and encourage each other verbally.

4. Conflict Management: When disagreements arise, commit to using "I" statements and maintain a respectful tone to instigate constructive resolutions.

The verbal connection in a Godly marriage is crucial to nurturing a strong, healthy relationship. Through effective communication, words of affirmation, and constructive conflict resolution, couples like Paul and Karen can build an enduring verbal bond that reflects Christ's love in their partnership. A thriving verbal connection contributes significantly to emotional intimacy and spiritual unity, allowing couples to navigate life together with grace and understanding. We will revisit many of these concepts in more depth later in this book.

How Unity and Intimacy are Strengthened Through Conversation

Unity and intimacy in a marriage are strengthened by meaningful conversation. Research, statistics, and biblical principles have proven the significance of communication in building a deeper connection between spouses.

Research from the American Association for Marriage and Family Therapy reveals that over 60% of divorces cite communication issues as a significant factor. This statistic underscores the importance of nurturing open and honest communication for building a strong marital bond.

A 2018 study published in the journal Personal Relationships noted that couples who engage in deep, meaningful conversations report higher levels of relationship satisfaction. Engaging discussions create a sense of togetherness and understanding that binds spouses closer.

We can also search the scriptures to find a Biblical foundation for this concept in our marital relationship.

Ephesians 4:2-3: *"With all humility and gentleness, with patience, bearing with one another in love, eager to maintain the unity of the Spirit in the bond of peace."*

This verse stresses the importance of approaching conversations with humility and love, qualities vital to maintaining unity and intimacy in marriage. Open-hearted dialogue creates an environment where both partners feel safe to express their feelings.

James 1:19: *"Let every person be quick to hear, slow to speak, slow to anger."*

This principle of active listening encourages partners to engage thoughtfully in conversations. Being quick to hear allows for deeper understanding and empathy, which enhances the intimacy of the relationship. Couples can strengthen their emotional and spiritual bonds by practicing this principle.

Aside from looking at this through the lens of statistics or biblically, we can also find applications that will help strengthen our bond as a couple in our everyday lives as well.

Establishing regular date nights creates space for intentional conversations about both light-hearted and serious topics. These moments allow couples to reconnect on various levels.

Teaching couples conflict resolution techniques can help them navigate disagreements effectively. Communication tools, such as "I" statements and reflective listening, can help mitigate the escalation of conflict.

Engaging in Bible study together encourages couples to discuss scripture and reflect on how biblical principles apply to their marriage. Sharing their insights creates unity and spiritual intimacy.

Unity and intimacy in marriage can be significantly enhanced through meaningful conversations. By integrating biblical insights and understanding the dynamics of effective communication, couples can cultivate deeper connections and a strengthened partnership grounded in faith.

Encouraging spouses to engage in active listening and open dialogue not only aligns with biblical teachings but reflects God's design for marriage, a partnership filled with love, understanding, and unity. Through intentional conversation, couples can cultivate a deeper emotional and spiritual bond.

At the lowest point in Michelle's and my marriage, we faced a reality that was both painful and disheartening. The unity we once cherished was shattered. Conflicts had become frequent, leaving emotional scars that hindered our connection. As disagreements piled up, the intimacy we had enjoyed faded away, replaced by misunderstandings, resentment, and silence. During this time, we found ourselves avoiding conversation like the plague.

The avoidance stemmed from a mixture of fear and fatigue. Conversations that had once been a source of joy became daunting reminders of our struggles. We hesitated to engage in dialogue, fearing that even the simplest discussions could ignite more conflict. This cycle perpetuated the distance between us, leading to deeper isolation within our relationship.

However, as we began working consciously on our marriage, we realized that rebuilding our unity and intimacy required a fundamental shift in our approach to conversation. Slowly, we began reintroducing meaningful dialogue into our relationship. We recognized that communication was not merely an exchange of words, but a crucial lifeline that would reconnect us.

In our journey towards reconnection, we applied four things in our marriage:

1. Intentional Conversations: We began to set aside time to talk, making an effort to create a safe space where both of us could share our thoughts and feelings. This shift was pivotal. It allowed us to express our frustrations, anecdotes from our days, and our dreams for the future without the weight of hostility.

2. Active Listening: We learned to practice active listening. Instead of waiting for our turn to speak, we intentionally focused on what the other was saying, seeking to understand their perspective. This practice helped us reconnect emotionally and opened pathways for greater intimacy.

3. Forgiveness and Grace: Central to our renewed conversations was the willingness to offer and seek forgiveness. Recognizing that we had both contributed to our struggles allowed us to extend grace to each other. We began to communicate not just with our words, but with our hearts.

4. Building Trust: With each open conversation, trust began to rebuild. We experienced the reassurance that came with vulnerability; sharing not just our thoughts but also our fears and hopes strengthened our emotional bond.

As unity and intimacy returned, we watched the quality of our conversations blossom. Topics shifted from mere logistics and daily stresses to deeper explorations of our values, aspirations, and spiritual journeys. We rediscovered the joy of sharing dreams and even of discussing disagreements constructively. By redirecting our focus to meaningful conversation, we not only healed our marriage but also nurtured a relationship marked by love, respect, and ongoing communication.

It's a reminder that while the road to healing may be challenging, embracing open, heartfelt dialogue can restore unity and deepen intimacy within a marriage, transforming a once-broken relationship into one that thrives on sincerity and love.

Speaking Life: Aligning Your Words with God's Heart

Speaking life and aligning our words with God's heart is a concept that holds transformative potential for married couples. At its core, this idea revolves around the understanding that our words possess significant power, both to build up and to tear down. In the context of marriage, aligning our speech with divine principles can lead to a relationship marked by mutual respect, love, and encouragement.

To speak life in a marriage means intentionally using our words to instigate positivity, understanding, and connection. Scripture highlights the importance of our speech in Proverbs 18:21, which states, *"Death and life are in the power of the tongue."* This verse emphasizes that the way we communicate can significantly impact our relationships, either nurturing them or creating barriers. When couples commit to speaking life into one another, they cultivate an environment where love flourishes, and unity is strengthened.

Aligning our words with God's heart begins with an awareness of the values and truths found in Scripture. God's heart reflects kindness, compassion, forgiveness, and encouragement. These attributes can shape our conversations, guiding us to choose words that reflect these qualities. For instance, expressing appreciation for one another, celebrating successes, or acknowledging each other's feelings can deepen intimacy and reinforce the bond between partners. When we intentionally speak words of affirmation and encouragement, we create a safe space for vulnerability and emotional connection.

Practical application of this principle can manifest in daily interactions. Couples might begin by practicing gratitude, taking time regularly to express what they appreciate about each other. This can be as simple as recognizing efforts in household responsibilities or appreciating the small, everyday gestures that often go unnoticed. These moments of acknowledgment can lay the foundation for a more sincere and fulfilling dialogue.

Additionally, it is crucial for couples to be mindful of their tone and delivery. Effective communication is not just about the words we choose, but also about how we deliver them. A gentle and loving tone can convey understanding, even when discussing complex topics. Conversely, harsh or critical words can create walls and provoke defensiveness, leading to misunderstandings. Therefore, being conscious of how we communicate, along with what we speak, becomes vital in aligning our words with God's heart.

Furthermore, conflict is an inevitable aspect of any marriage, but how couples navigate disagreements can either hinder or enhance their connection. Rather than resorting to hurtful words during disagreements, couples can benefit from employing "I" statements to express their feelings without placing blame. For example, saying "I feel hurt when..." rather than accusing, generates healthier discussion and opens the door to resolution. By practicing this kind of thoughtful communication, couples can demonstrate love and respect even amidst challenges.

Another practical approach involves praying together as a couple. Inviting God into your discussions not only aligns your heart with His but also creates an atmosphere of humility and reconciliation. Prayer can serve as a guide for both partners to express desires for understanding and

growth, allowing the couple to align their hearts and words with God's will.

Speaking life and aligning our words with God's heart are essential practices that can breathe new life into marital relationships. Couples who commit to this approach will find that their words can uplift, encourage, and nurture intimacy. By intentionally choosing kind, affirming language, being mindful of communication styles, handling conflicts with grace, and seeking guidance through prayer, partners create a marriage grounded in love and respect. Ultimately, aligning words with God's heart allows married couples to reflect the very nature of Christ in their relationship, leading to flourishing and enduring unity.

The Spiritual Battle Against Communication Breakdowns

Communication breakdowns within a marriage often go beyond mere misunderstandings; they can become a spiritual battle influenced by external forces seeking to undermine the sacred union between spouses. As believers, we recognize that our relationships are not just grounded in the physical realm but are also influenced by spiritual dynamics at play, particularly in the context of marriage, which reflects Christ's relationship with the Church (Ephesians 5:25).

Satan, as described in John 10:10, seeks to *"steal, kill, and destroy,"* and he targets the very fabric of our marriages through the words we use and the manner in which we communicate. When conflict arises, it is often accompanied by frustration, anger, and, at times, bitterness. In these moments, the enemy may whisper lies that lead to negative self-talk and destructive dialogue between partners. For instance, a spouse may recite a narrative of inadequacy or frustration, exacerbating conflicts rather than promoting understanding. This inner turmoil can distort how we express ourselves, leading to harsh words, critical tones, and a lack of empathy.

This communication breakdown can create a breeding ground for resentment and division. As couples allow negative speech patterns to define their interactions, unity erodes. Instead of working through conflicts collaboratively, they can fall into patterns of avoidance or blame, which drives a wedge further into their relationship. In essence, these communication failures become a spiritual battleground where the peace and oneness God desires for married couples are challenged.

To combat these spiritual attacks, it is vital for couples to be prepared and equipped to fight against the tendencies that lead to communication breakdowns. The first step involves recognizing that our words hold power (Proverbs 18:21). With this awareness, couples can become vigilant in monitoring how they speak to one another, intentionally choosing language that uplifts, encourages connection, and avoids division.

Couples need to prioritize establishing an atmosphere of grace and understanding in their conversations. This involves not only being mindful of their words but also cultivating a heart of forgiveness and humility. When arguments arise, they should approach each other with the intent to listen actively and seek understanding, rather than react defensively. Engaging in prayers for wisdom and insight during discussions invites God's presence into the conversation, helping both spouses realign their hearts with His purpose for their relationship.

Additionally, couples can prepare spiritually by committing to daily prayer together. This practice creates a powerful bond, grounding their marriage in prayer and inviting God's strength into their interactions. It reminds them of their shared commitment to one another and reinforces the idea that their struggles are not just personal but part of a broader spiritual warfare.

Furthermore, equipping themselves with Scripture can also provide couples with a foundation for their dialogue. Verses that emphasize love, kindness, humility, and patience become touchstones that guide their discussions and remind them of their commitment to each other and to God. For instance, reflecting on Colossians 3:12-14, which calls for compassion and forgiveness, frames conversations in a light of grace and mutual support, allowing couples to view their challenges through a spiritual lens.

Communication breakdowns in marriage are not merely relational; they can be viewed as a spiritual battle. Satan seeks to exploit misunderstandings and conflicts to weaken the bond between spouses. By recognizing the spiritual implications of their conversations and preparing to counteract these attacks with prayer, intentionality, and Scripture, couples can overcome communication barriers. This proactive approach not only enhances their dialogue but ultimately fortifies their marriage, allowing them to experience the unity and intimacy God desires for their relationship. By aligning their words with God's heart and purpose, couples can turn potential points of conflict into opportunities for growth, healing, and stronger bonds.

As we reflect on the power of our words and the importance of speaking life into our marriages, it becomes clear that effective communication is not solely about what we say but also about how we engage with each other. The next crucial element in cultivating unity and intimacy is the art of listening, a skill that has, in many ways, been overshadowed in our fast-paced, distraction-laden world. Listening is more than just hearing words; it requires intentionality and vulnerability. It calls us to pay close attention not only to our partner's spoken words but also to their emotions, body language, and underlying needs. As we jump into the next chapter, we will explore listening as a vital component of marriage, understanding how the lost art of paying attention can transform our conversations, deepen our connections, and empower us to truly know and love each other as God intended. In doing so, we will uncover practical steps to enhance our listening skills and engage more meaningfully in our relationships, paving the way for that unity and intimacy in our marriage that is so essential to our relationship.

Chapter Two

Listening Like Jesus: The Lost Art of Paying Attention

Biblical Foundation: James 1:19, Proverbs 1:5, Luke 24:15–17

I n our fast-paced, distraction-filled world, the art of listening seems to be fading into obscurity. After all, how many times have we found ourselves physically present with our spouse, while our minds wander off to a distant galaxy? To illustrate this, let's share an interaction between Paul and Janice.

Janice, armed with enthusiasm and a list of updates from her day, approaches Paul, who is comfortably settled on the couch, remote in one hand and a snack in the other. As she opens up about her day at work, detailing the chaotic office antics involving a missing stapler and an ill-fated cake mix disaster, Paul is nodding along. However, his eyes remain glued to the television screen. Unbeknownst to him, he's entered what we might call "selective listening mode." His half-hearted responses of "uh-huh" and "interesting" are outgoing, while the internal dialogue in his mind might very well be narrating the dramatic finale of the game he's watching.

Janice, sensing that her riveting tale of workplace mischief isn't landing quite as intended, humorously quips, "You know, honey, I'm not sure if you're listening to me or just rooting for your team's mascot at this point!" This playful jab serves a dual purpose: it injects humor into the moment while simultaneously illuminating a deeper truth about the importance of fully engaging in conversation. Unfortunately, this scenario is all too common; people often find themselves multitasking, mentally tuned out, or prioritizing distractions over genuine connection.

The reality is that in the sacred space of marriage, where intimacy and understanding thrive, listening must take precedence over mere hearing. Without active listening, we risk building walls that create distance rather than bridges that invite closeness. In the subsequent sections, we'll explore practical steps to rekindle this lost art, ensuring that partners like Paul and Janice don't just occupy the same room but fully inhabit the shared journey of their lives together. After all, as we will see, listening goes beyond the absence of noise – it requires commitment, intentionality, and most importantly, love.

Why Listening is the Foundation of Truly Being Heard

Listening, especially within the context of marriage, is not simply a passive act; it's an art that requires skill and intentionality. Yet the statistics reveal a sobering truth about how we typically engage in conversations with our spouses. Research suggests that the average spouse listens for only about 14 seconds during a conflict conversation before feeling compelled to interject their opinion or response. This alarming statistic reveals a broader issue in relationships: that many of us prioritize our own voices over the vital act of genuinely hearing our partners.

Consider studies conducted by the University of Washington, which indicate that during conflicts, individuals tend to interrupt their partners an average of 4 times for every time their partner interrupts. This can lead to a cycle of miscommunication and frustration, creating an en-

vironment where feelings of being unheard permeate the relationship. Furthermore, the American Psychological Association reports that couples who engage in active listening, where one partner reflects on what was said before responding, display significantly lower rates of conflict and higher levels of relationship satisfaction. Yet, despite this knowledge, many of us find it challenging to pause, reflect, and respond thoughtfully in the moment.

Why do we struggle so much with authentic listening? In today's information-overloaded society, our attention spans are shrinking. A study by Microsoft Corporation found that the average person's attention span is now shorter than that of a goldfish, clocking in at about 8 seconds. This reality impacts our relationships, as we often approach conversations with our spouses distractedly, multitasking or thinking ahead to how we intend to respond rather than fully engaging with the moment. It's no wonder that conversations can become battlegrounds rather than safe spaces for empathy and connection.

To add another layer of complexity, societal pressures and individual stressors can contribute to our inability to listen well. In times of emotional turmoil or when faced with interpersonal conflicts, our instinct often shifts towards defense and self-preservation. The result? Critical moments of connection are overshadowed by our need to be heard rather than our willingness to listen.

Listening is not merely a passive activity; it is the essential foundation for effective communication and mutual understanding in any relationship, particularly within the sacred space of marriage. The dynamics of being truly heard hinge on the depth of listening in conversations. Studies consistently demonstrate that when individuals genuinely listen to their partners, it not only increases feelings of connection but also creates emotional intimacy, trust, and empathy, crucial elements for a thriving marriage.

One fundamental reason why listening is foundational to being heard is that it creates an environment where partners feel valued and respected. Research published in the journal *"Personal Relationships"* highlights that effective listening helps validate one's feelings and experiences. When one spouse actively listens, laying aside distractions, maintaining eye contact, and offering affirming nonverbal cues, they communicate that their partner's thoughts and feelings matter. This validation is essential; as humans, we crave recognition and understanding from those closest to us. Without it, conversations can often devolve into frustration and misunderstanding.

Furthermore, listening enhances clarity and reduces the potential for conflict. A study published in the *"Journal of Marriage and Family"* found that couples who used active listening techniques, such as summarizing what the other person said or asking clarifying questions, reported feeling more satisfied with their conversations and were better equipped to resolve disagreements. Active listening can help couples navigate difficult discussions more constructively, allowing them to focus on understanding each other's perspectives rather than merely formulating their next response.

The implications of listening extend beyond individual conversations; they influence the overall health of the relationship. According to a survey from the American Association for Marriage and Family Therapy, couples who prioritize effective communication, which includes active listening, experience higher rates of relationship satisfaction and stability. By creating an environment of open dialogue, couples fortify their emotional connection and build resilience against external pressures and internal conflicts.

In practical terms, mastering the art of listening means setting aside time for undistracted conversations, asking meaningful questions, and responding with empathy. It empowers partners to address their needs and resolve misunderstandings while simultaneously deepening their relational bond. Ultimately, the ability to listen well transforms conversations from routine exchanges into opportunities for growth, connection, and mutual respect. As couples learn to prioritize listening as an integral part of their communication, they pave the way for a marriage rooted in love, understanding, and shared experience, a true testament to the transformative power of truly being heard.

The Difference Between Hearing and Active, Empathetic Listening

Typical hearing and active empathetic listening are two distinctly different approaches to communication that significantly impact the quality of interactions, especially in close relationships such as marriage. Hearing, in its most basic form, is a physiological process, the perception of sound waves through the ear. While we may hear our partner's words, this does not guarantee that we are truly processing or understanding their message. In fact, typical hearing often involves passive acknowledgment, where an individual may nod or make brief comments without fully engaging with the content or emotion behind the words. This can lead to misunderstandings, frustration, and a sense of disconnection, as one partner may feel their thoughts and feelings are being overlooked or dismissed.

In contrast, active empathetic listening requires deliberate effort and skill. It goes beyond merely hearing the words; it involves focusing entirely on the speaker, understanding their perspective, and responding with empathy. This means not only listening to what is being said but also attuning to nonverbal cues, such as body language and tone of voice. Active listening entails reflecting what has been said, validating emotions, and asking clarifying questions, creating a space where both partners feel acknowledged and understood. Research has shown that couples who practice active, empathetic listening report higher levels of relationship satisfaction, as it promotes deeper emotional intimacy and a sense of safety when sharing vulnerable thoughts.

The difference between these two approaches can significantly influence how couples communicate during conflicts or stressful moments. Where typical hearing might lead to interruptions or defensive responses, active empathetic listening cultivates patience and a commitment to truly understanding one another. This not only diminishes the likelihood of escalation during disagreements but also builds trust, partners feel more secure in sharing their thoughts because they know they are genuinely heard. As couples develop the habit of active listening, they lay the foundation for deeper connections and a more resilient relationship, ultimately transforming their conversations from mere exchanges of words to meaningful dialogues filled with compassion and understanding.

You may be asking, *"How do I put active listening into practice in my marriage?"* Well, I'm glad you asked! Putting active listening into practice with your spouse involves intentional efforts to create a supportive environment for meaningful conversation. Here are several practical steps that can help strengthen this essential skill and enhance communication within your relationship:

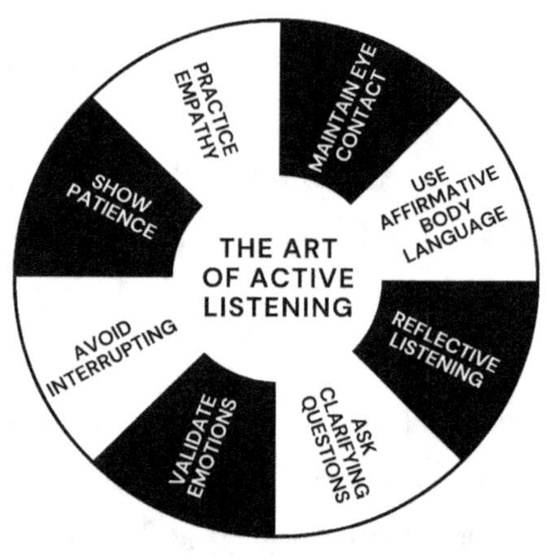

1. Create a Distraction-Free Environment: To engage in active listening, it's essential to minimize distractions. Set aside dedicated time to talking when both partners are undistracted by televisions, smartphones, or other interruptions. Choose a comfortable setting where you can focus on each other.

2. Maintain Eye Contact: Eye contact is a powerful nonverbal cue that signifies your engagement and commitment to listening. It helps convey that you are present and genuinely interested in what your spouse is sharing. Leaning slightly towards them can also demonstrate your attentiveness.

3. Use Affirmative Body Language: Nodding your head, leaning slightly forward, and maintaining an open posture can communicate to your spouse that you are actively engaged. These nonverbal signals of interest can encourage them to express themselves more fully.

4. Practice Reflective Listening: After your partner finishes speaking, paraphrase what they've said to ensure clarity and demonstrate understanding. For example, you might say, "What I hear you saying is that you felt frustrated when..." This not only validates their feelings but also ensures that you accurately grasp their perspective.

5. Ask Clarifying Questions: To deepen your understanding, ask open-ended questions that encourage your spouse to elaborate on their thoughts and feelings. For instance, "How did that make you feel?" or "Can you tell me more about what you were thinking?" These prompts invite exploration instead of simple yes/no responses.

6. Validate Their Emotions: Let your spouse know that their feelings are valid and understandable, even if you don't fully agree with their viewpoint. Statements like "I can see why you'd feel that way" or "That sounds really tough" can create an atmosphere of empathy and connection.

7. Avoid Interrupting or Formulating Responses Prematurely: Resist the urge to jump in with your own opinions or solutions while your spouse is speaking. Allow them to express their thoughts before you respond. This can be challenging, especially during heated discussions, but it's crucial for effective listening.

8. Show Patience: Active listening requires time. Allow your spouse to express themselves fully without rushing the conversation. Be patient and resist the temptation to move on to the next topic until they've finished sharing.

9. Provide Thoughtful Responses: Once your spouse has finished speaking, reflect on their comments and respond thoughtfully. Share your perspective or feelings while acknowledging what they shared. This mutual exchange encourages deeper connection and understanding.

10. Practice Empathy: Make a genuine effort to put yourself in your spouse's shoes. Understanding their emotions and perspective allows you to respond with compassion, thereby strengthening your emotional bond.

By intentionally incorporating these steps into their interactions, couples can create a stronger sense of connection and understanding in their conversations. Active listening not only enhances communication but also strengthens trust, empathy, and emotional intimacy, laying a vital foundation for a healthy, thriving marriage.

Slowing Down and Creating Emotional Space for Your Spouse

In the hustle and bustle of our microwave society, it is all too easy to fall into the trap of hurried conversations, where words are exchanged but genuine connection is lost. Slowing down and creating emotional space for your spouse during conversations is not just a luxury but a necessity for maintaining intimacy and understanding. When couples pause to listen to one another genuinely, they cultivate an environment where both partners feel valued and heard. This mindful approach invites a deeper exploration of thoughts and emotions, paving the way for richer conversations that strengthen relational bonds.

The differences in how men and women communicate can significantly influence the dynamics of these conversations. Research suggests that women often value connection and emotional depth in communication. They tend to seek understanding and validation through conversation, sharing experiences and feelings in a way that invites intimacy. Men, on the other hand, may approach conversations with a more solution-focused mindset. They might prioritize problem-solving and may interpret discussions as opportunities to offer advice or fix issues rather than purely as a way to share emotions. This fundamental difference can create friction if partners do not intentionally slow down and adjust their communication styles to meet each other's needs.

When one partner, often the wife, seeks emotional connection and shares feelings in an attempt to create closeness, while the other, often the husband, aims to resolve issues quickly, misunderstandings can arise. A woman might feel unheard or dismissed when her husband jumps straight to solutions instead of acknowledging her feelings. Conversely, the man may feel frustrated by what he perceives as a lack of practicality in his partner's approach. Recognizing and respecting these differences is key. By creating emotional space in conversations, couples allow each other the freedom to express feelings without the immediate pressure to respond or rectify the situation.

One effective way to create this emotional space is to practice active listening. This means deliberately taking the time to fully understand what your spouse is saying before reacting. It involves refraining from interrupting, validating feelings, and asking open-ended questions that encourage exploration. For example, a husband might take a deep breath and listen attentively as his wife shares her day's challenges, resisting the urge to offer solutions immediately. Instead, he could respond with something like, "It sounds like you had a really tough day. I'm here for you. Tell me more about what happened." Such a response not only affirms her emotions but also conveys a willingness to be present, ensuring that both partners feel connected and understood.

Additionally, establishing agreed-upon "listening moments" can help couples to slow down, creating designated times where each person can speak freely without interruption. This practice can allow for greater emotional sharing, strengthening the relational foundation. As partners embrace this intentionality in their conversations, they find their emotional connection deepening. Respecting each other's needs, recognizing communication differences, and creating space to listen genuinely promotes an environment where both partners feel safe and valued, ultimately transforming conversations into powerful tools for connection, intimacy, and love.

Asking Questions that Draw Out the Heart

Heart talk is a term for engaging in deep, meaningful conversations that connect partners on an emotional and spiritual level. It transcends the surface-level exchanges that often characterize daily interactions and invites couples to share their innermost feelings, thoughts, and desires. Integrated into good communication with your spouse, heart talk promotes understanding, empathy, and intimacy by providing a safe space for vulnerability. This level of communication goes beyond mere listening; it encompasses the commitment to truly understand and connect with each other's experiences and emotional landscapes.

At the core of heart talk is the recognition that communication is not just about exchanging information but also about nurturing the bond between partners. When couples engage in heart talk, they prioritize emotional honesty and openness, allowing them to explore each other's feelings in a supportive environment. This can involve sharing hopes, fears, dreams, and even regrets, essentially everything that fuels their individual identities and their shared relationship. Heart talk can serve as a powerful antidote to the isolation that often creeps into relationships over time, encouraging a sense of closeness and understanding.

One essential aspect of heart talk is asking good, deep questions. These questions are designed to elicit thoughtful responses and promote exploration into one's emotions and beliefs. Instead of sticking to small talk or transactional dialogue, deep questions help uncover layer after layer of what truly matters to each partner. For example, instead of asking, *"How was your day?"* a more probing question could be, *"Was there any moment that was the highlight of your day? What was the low of your day?"* This type of inquiry encourages reflection and invites each partner to share feelings or thoughts that may otherwise remain hidden beneath the surface.

Asking good, deep questions within the framework of heart talk not only draws out your spouse's heart but also demonstrates genuine interest and care for their inner world. It creates opportunities for partners to articulate their values, dreams, and struggles, resulting in richer conversations that strengthen their connection. For instance, asking questions like *"What are your biggest fears about our future together?"* or *"What do you wish we could explore as a couple?"* can lead to impactful discussions that shape the relationship's trajectory.

Heart talk, therefore, serves as more than a communication strategy; it becomes a powerful tool for transformation in relationships. By focusing on emotional connection, practicing vulnerability, and embracing deep questioning, couples can cultivate a more fulfilling partnership, enhancing their understanding of one another and deepening their love. As spouses grow comfortable with each other's heart talk, they step into a space where their relationship can flourish, rooted in authenticity, trust, and a sincere appreciation for the complexities that each partner brings to the union.

Heart talk can be a powerful conduit for intimacy and understanding in a marriage, but it inherently requires the active participation of both partners. If one spouse is unwilling to listen actively or lacks sincerity during these conversations, the effectiveness of heart talk diminishes

significantly. Listening is not merely about hearing words; it's about creating an emotional environment where both partners feel valued, understood, and safe to express their innermost thoughts and feelings.

When a partner approaches heart talk without genuine interest or engagement, it creates an unsettling dynamic that can undermine the very foundation upon which these conversations are built. For instance, if one spouse is distracted, dismissive, or quick to judge, the other may feel vulnerable and exposed yet simultaneously unheard. This immediate mismatch in openness and engagement can provoke feelings of frustration, isolation, and apprehension. Instead of facilitating deeper connections, heart talk can devolve into superficial exchanges, marked by surface-level responses and unmet emotional needs.

Furthermore, when one partner fails to listen actively, it can create a sense of emotional unsafety that stifles honest dialogue. A spouse who perceives that their feelings are not being valued may become reluctant to share deeper emotions in the future, fearing that vulnerability could be met with indifference or criticism. This results in a vicious cycle, lack of sincere listening leads to guarded expressions, which, in turn, inform a decreasing willingness to engage in heart talk altogether. Over time, this can create emotional distance, as partners may retreat into silence or develop a habit of avoiding significant conversations altogether, feeling that their voice carries little weight in the relationship.

For heart talk to flourish, it demands a commitment to active listening and sincerity from both partners. This means not only hearing each other's words but also being attuned to the underlying emotions and desires that drive those conversations. Couples must cultivate an atmosphere of empathy, where they approach heart talk as an opportunity to understand one another deeply rather than as a checklist or a transactional dialogue.

Ultimately, for heart talk to be successful, both partners must take responsibility for their engagement in the conversation. They need to create an emotional space where vulnerability is met with acceptance, where genuine listening reinforces the desire to be heard, and where love, trust, and respect form the solid foundation upon which deep connections can thrive. Without this mutual commitment, the potential for heart talk is diminished, and the relationship risks becoming emotionally stagnant, lacking the richness and depth that comes from truly engaging with each other's hearts.

During the early days of our marriage, Michelle and I were like two ships passing in the night. We were both excited to set out on this new voyage together, yet we were unprepared for the storms that loomed on the horizon. Each of us brought our own baggage onto the ship, past hurts, unresolved conflicts, and miscommunication. These burdens were like invisible anchors, weighing down our vessels and preventing us from navigating the waters of intimacy and understanding.

In those days, our conversations often felt like a series of surface-level exchanges, weather reports and grocery lists, rather than deep, meaningful heart talks. We failed to communicate our feelings and needs truly. When misunderstandings arose, instead of addressing them directly, we withdrew, allowing resentment to build like tumultuous waves crashing against our ship. It wasn't long before these waves culminated in a severe crisis that brought us to the brink of divorce.

It was a dark season, filled with arguments and silences, where love felt more like duty than delight. We were adrift, and our marriage seemed almost beyond repair. But it was in that very darkness that we found the light, we realized that without heart talk, without vulnerability, we could not heal.

Together, we decided to confront our past baggage and the miscommunication that had haunted us. We invested time and energy in learning how to open our hearts and speak honestly about our feelings, fears, and expectations. We began setting aside regular time for meaningful conversation, creating a safe space where each of us could express ourselves without judgment.

Gradually, we learned to listen, affirm, and empathize. It was like raising the anchor that had held us back, allowing us to navigate toward healing. As we embraced this new practice of heart talk, our communication began to flourish. Clarity replaced confusion, and connection emerged from chaos.

Now, our relationship is not just surviving; it's thriving. The storms of the past have equipped us with resilience, and the sails of honest communication now guide our ship. We have discovered that heart talk isn't merely about exchanging words; it's about crafting a deeper bond that reflects the grace and love God intends for marriage.

We learned that understanding and transparency can transform even the most troubled waters into a journey of growth and intimacy. By exchanging our baggage for heartfelt conversations, we've found a way to navigate the seas of our life together, anchored in love and understanding.

Eliminating Distraction: Being Present in a Noisy World

In today's fast-paced society, we are bombarded with distractions that creep into every aspect of our lives, including our most intimate relationships. The ubiquitous presence of devices, smartphones, tablets, laptops, has transformed the way we communicate, often relegating face-to-face conversations to secondary status. Notifications pinging for messages, social media updates, and entertainment options constantly vie for our attention, making it increasingly challenging to connect authentically. This constant influx of distractions contributes to a disconnect in our marriages, as spouses are often physically present but emotionally distant, spending more time on screens than together.

Televisions play their own role in diverting attention within households. How many evenings do couples spend in the same room, but with one partner absorbed in a show while the other scrolls through their phone? This scenario, while comfortable in its familiarity, operates on a paradox: although we may be sharing physical space, we are simultaneously creating emotional distance. There is a growing body of research indicating that multitasking during conversations leads to poorer communication outcomes, with individuals failing to grasp each other's emotional expressions and opinions fully. The irony is that, while technology is designed to connect us with the broader world, it often disconnects us from our partners right beside us.

Additionally, societal pressures, long work hours, and mounting stress can compound these distractions. When spouses come home after a long day, the tendency is often to retreat into personal devices as a means of escape or relaxation, inadvertently sidelining the critical need for intentional, meaningful conversation. This can lead to feelings of isolation, frustration, and even resentment, as neither partner feels heard or valued in the relationship. Over time, these minor disconnections can erode the foundation of intimacy, leading to a marriage that feels more like cohabitation than a partnership.

To combat these distractions and create a more connected relationship, couples can implement several key solutions aimed at re-establishing presence and emotional intimacy:

1. Designate Device-Free Times: Establish specific times during the day or week when all devices are put away. This could be during meals, before bedtime, or designated "date nights." The absence of distractions allows couples to focus solely on each other, promoting deeper conversations and shared experiences.

2. Create a Welcoming Home Environment: Transform communal spaces to encourage connection. Set up cozy areas geared towards conversation, such as a comfortable nook for coffee in the morning, free of screens. This physical space can create an emotional space conducive to heart talk.

3. Practice Intentional Listening: Prioritize active listening in conversations by maintaining eye contact and setting aside time to engage in meaningful discussions. Use reflective listening techniques to show understanding and empathy, ensuring your partner feels heard and valued.

4. Establish Weekly Check-ins: Schedule regular times every week to openly discuss feelings, aspirations, or concerns. These check-ins can be a safe space for both partners to express themselves without fear of judgment or interruption, rediscovering the intimacy that may have been lost.

5. Limit Television Usage: While watching TV can be a way of unwinding, it should not replace conversations. Opt for shows that ignite discussions or watch together with a shared intent, making it a way to bond rather than a barrier.

6. Mindfulness Practices: Incorporate mindfulness into your relationship, encouraging both partners to be present. Brief moments of silence, meditation, or deep breathing can ground the conversation and enhance emotional connections.

In a noisy world filled with distractions, the goal is to cultivate a marriage that prioritizes connection over convenience. By implementing these strategies, couples can reclaim their communication and create an environment where love, understanding, and intimacy can flourish. Such intentional actions will bridge the gap created by distractions and lead to a deeper, more fulfilling relationship, where partners feel truly seen, heard, and valued amidst the noise of modern life.

Listen Like Jesus

Listening like Jesus means engaging in communication characterized by presence, empathy, and a genuine desire to understand others. Throughout the Gospel accounts, we find numerous examples of Jesus exemplifying this deep, compassionate listening, an approach we are called to emulate in our relationships, particularly in marriage. Jesus's ability to listen and respond thoughtfully demonstrates the powerful impact of active listening on personal connections.

In the Gospels, Jesus often made Himself available to others, prioritizing relationships over distractions. For example, in Mark 10:46-52, we read about Bartimaeus, a blind beggar who cried out to Jesus as He passed by. Despite the crowd urging Bartimaeus to be silent, Jesus stopped and asked, *"What do you want me to do for you?"* This moment illustrates the importance of creating emotional space in our conversations. Jesus did not rush; instead, He paused to listen to Bartimaeus's needs and desires. He was fully present at that moment, which validated Bartimaeus's worth and need for attention. This illustrates to us that, in our marriages, we must create and honor moments to fully understand our spouse's heart and needs.

Additionally, in John 4, Jesus' encounter with the Samaritan woman at the well provides an excellent example of how He actively listened and engaged in heart talk. Despite societal norms that dictated otherwise, Jesus took the time to converse with her, asking probing questions and affirming her identity beyond the surface level. He listened to her story, acknowledging her struggles before revealing His own identity as the living water. Through this dialogue, He demonstrated that effective communication requires more than just exchanging words; it demands a willingness to explore into the complexities of another person's experience. This is particularly relevant in marital communication, where partners must strive to understand each other's deeper stories without judgment.

In Matthew 7:12, often called the "Golden Rule," Jesus taught us to treat others as we wish to be treated. This principle can be applied to how we listen; we should aim to give our spouses the genuine listening and attention we ourselves desire. When we engage in conversations, especially during conflicts, we must strive to embody empathy and respect rather than defensiveness. By genuinely listening to our spouse's concerns and feelings, just as we would hope they would listen to ours, we create an environment of mutual support and understanding.

The ripple effects of such considerate communication can significantly enhance marital intimacy. Ephesians 4:29 encourages us to let no unwholesome talk come out of our mouths, but only what helps build others up according to their needs. By implementing Jesus' model of listening, where we demonstrate patience, love, and a desire to uplift each other, we can transform our daily interactions into opportunities that create deeper connections and emotionally nourishing dialogues.

To listen like Jesus is to actively and compassionately engage in conversation with others. It involves being genuinely present, asking meaningful questions, and demonstrating an unwavering commitment to understanding. By following His example of compassionate listening, we can establish and nurture healthy communication patterns within our marriages, leading not only to personal growth and deeper intimacy but also to communities that reflect the love and grace that Jesus exemplified. Listening in this way is essential for building strong, loving relationships grounded in respect, understanding, and emotional connection.

Chapter Three

The Power of Communication in Marriage

Biblical Foundation: James 1:19, Colossians 4:6

Communication is often called the lifeblood of any relationship, and in marriage, it plays a particularly vital role. Just as a sturdy foundation is essential for a house to stand, the way we communicate forms the bedrock of our marital relationship. Unfortunately, this foundation can be vulnerable, subject to the weight of past experiences and emotional baggage we may carry into our unions. When miscommunication or silence takes root, it can erode trust and understanding, leading to misunderstandings that tear down even the strongest bonds.

In our journey as couples, the words we choose and the way we express ourselves can either constructively build up our relationship or destructively undermine it. In the beginning, it's often easy to be enamored with one another, but as time goes on, the challenges of daily life can introduce discord. We may find ourselves speaking in terms of complaints rather than affirmations or engaging in conversations that fail to address the deeper emotional needs we each have. Left unaddressed, these patterns can spiral into conflict, isolation, and ultimately, disconnection.

Yet there is hope. If we recognize the power of open, honest heart talks and commit to creating an environment where vulnerability is welcomed, we can transform our communication habits. Through intentional dialogue and active listening, we can lay a foundation that not only withstands the storms of life but also cultivates a deeper intimacy in our relationships. This chapter will explore the crucial role of communication in shaping our marriages, and how we can harness its potential to build stronger, more resilient connections with our partners. In doing so, we will learn that the words we speak, and the silence we sometimes maintain, shape the narrative of our love story in important ways.

Balancing Honesty with Kindness

Balancing honesty with kindness is pivotal in any marital relationship, serving as the dual pillars that support a healthy, enduring partnership. Honesty cultivates trust and openness, allowing couples to communicate their true feelings, needs, and concerns. It enables spouses to confront difficult topics and share vulnerabilities, crucial for building intimacy and understanding. However, honesty alone, without the tempering influence of kindness, can lead to hurt feelings and unnecessary conflict.

When honesty is expressed without kindness, the truth can become a weapon rather than a tool for growth. For instance, one spouse might share a critical observation about their partner's behavior, but if it is delivered harshly or insensitively, it can feel more like an attack than con-

structive feedback. This not only damages the recipient's self-esteem but can also create an environment of defensiveness and resentment, where open communication is stifled, and both partners feel threatened.

On the other hand, kindness without honesty can lead to stagnation in a marriage. If one spouse continually suppresses their true feelings or avoids difficult conversations to maintain a facade of harmony, it often results in unresolved issues and buried resentments. The intention may be to protect the other's feelings, but in reality, this can cultivate a climate of insecurity and mistrust. The sidelining of important discussions can accumulate communication barriers, causing partners to drift apart emotionally over time as unaddressed concerns fester beneath the surface.

The balance between honesty and kindness is therefore essential for effective communication. It allows spouses to voice their truths while ensuring those truths are delivered in a way that uplifts and nurtures the relationship. When both elements coexist, they create an atmosphere where vulnerability is welcomed, enabling heart-to-heart conversations that encourage growth and unity. This balance enables couples to navigate conflicts more effectively, reinforcing their love and commitment while empowering each partner to feel heard, valued, and respected.

In essence, failing to maintain this balance can lead to a breakdown in communication and intimacy, paving the way for distance and disconnect. When honesty is expressed carelessly or kindness is offered without sincerity, the foundations of mutual respect and understanding begin to erode, ultimately threatening the very essence of the marital bond. Therefore, cultivating a practice that emphasizes both honesty and kindness is not just beneficial but essential for a thriving, resilient marriage.

How Tone, Timing, and Delivery Shape What Your Spouse Feels

In any conversation, particularly in the context of marriage, the effectiveness of communication is significantly influenced by three critical factors: tone, timing, and delivery. Each of these elements can shape how a spouse perceives the message and, ultimately, how they feel about the discussion.

Tone refers to the emotional quality conveyed by the voice, ranging from warmth and affection to irritation or anger. For instance, a gentle or supportive tone can create a sense of safety and openness, encouraging honest dialogue. Conversely, a harsh or sarcastic tone can create defensiveness and hurt, even if the words themselves are not overtly critical.

Timing involves choosing the right moment to initiate a conversation. Addressing sensitive issues during a high-stress moment, such as after a long day or while one partner is distracted, can hinder effective communication. On the other hand, engaging in conversation when both partners are calm and present allows for a more thoughtful exchange and a greater likelihood of understanding.

Delivery encompasses the overall manner in which a message is communicated, including body language, facial expressions, and word choice. A thoughtful, respectful delivery can enhance the message, making it well-received, while an insensitive or dismissive manner can detract from the content.

Together, **tone**, **timing**, and **delivery** create the framework within which words are interpreted. Understanding and intentionally managing these aspects can lead to healthier, more constructive conversations, initiating a deeper emotional connection between spouses. In the following sections, we will break down each of these factors to explore how they specifically impact communication in marriage and provide practical strategies for improving them.

Tone

Tone plays a crucial role in shaping how messages are received in conversations between spouses. It conveys emotions and intentions that words alone may not fully express. Therefore, the difference between a good tone and a bad tone can significantly affect how the message is interpreted and the overall emotional climate of the conversation.

Examples of Good Tone:

Using my wife, Michelle, and myself as an example, let's say Michelle has had a long day at work and comes home feeling stressed. When discussing dinner plans, I ask her, "How about something quick and easy tonight? I know you've had a long day."

If Michelle responds with a calm and appreciative tone, saying, "That sounds great! Thanks for being so understanding," it creates warmth and connection. My kind and supportive approach makes it safe for Michelle to express her feelings. The positive tone creates an atmosphere where both of us feel valued and understood, allowing for open and fruitful communication.

Example of Bad Tone

In contrast, consider a similar scenario where Michelle comes home exhausted. I ask about dinner plans, and she says she's tired and doesn't know what to fix for dinner. Then I respond in a hateful way, and instead of being gentle, I say, "Why can't you just decide for once? It's not that hard!"

Here, my tone is sharp and condescending, which triggers defensiveness in Michelle. Instead of feeling supported, Michelle may feel attacked and respond with frustration or withdrawal. This negative tone shuts down communication and can deepen rifts between us, leading to further misunderstandings.

These examples reveal the significant impact of tone on communication within a relationship. A positive, understanding tone instigates connection and openness, while a negative tone can lead to defensiveness and distance. Recognizing how we communicate with one another is vital to nurturing a healthy, supportive relationship.

Making Our Connection Better with Good Tone:

1. Practice Mindfulness: Being aware of our tone during conversations is essential. Before speaking, spouses should take a moment to consider how their delivery may impact the other person. Practicing mindfulness can help us approach conversations more intentionally.

2. Use Affirmative Language: Incorporating affirming phrases and expressions can soften the tone and create a more welcoming atmosphere. Phrases like "I appreciate your input" or "I understand where you're coming from" signal respect and openness.

3. Empathize and Validate: When a spouse expresses feelings or frustrations, responding with understanding rather than judgment promotes a positive tone. For instance, instead of dismissing concerns by saying, "I can see why you're frustrated; let's work through this together," you model empathy.

4. Adjust Volume and Speed: Sometimes it's not just what we say but how we say it. Speaking slowly and softly can express gentleness and concern, while raising one's voice or speaking rapidly can convey anxiety or aggression. Being conscious of the volume and pace can greatly improve how the message is received.

5. Create a Safe Space for Dialogue: Establishing a dedicated time for "heart talks," where partners agree to engage in open conversations in a calm setting, can help ensure that tone remains positive. Making it a routine facilitates a supportive environment for discussions that matter.

By consciously nurturing a positive tone in conversations, couples can strengthen their connection, deepen understanding, and create a safe space for dialogue that encourages intimacy. It involves both intentionality in communication and a commitment to relational health, enabling partners to navigate the complexities of married life more effectively.

Timing

Effective communication in a marriage relies not only on the words we choose but also on the timing of our conversations. Establishing a good time for dialogue can significantly influence the outcome of those discussions, especially when emotions are involved. For Michelle and me, understanding when to approach certain topics enhances our connection and promotes a more intimate relationship.

The Importance of Timing

The timing of a conversation is crucial, particularly in sensitive or emotionally charged discussions. For instance, if Michelle has had a particularly stressful day at work and comes home visibly exhausted, it may not be the best time to discuss financial planning or household responsibilities. Instead, waiting until she has had some time to unwind, perhaps over dinner when both of us are relaxed, could create a more conducive environment for open dialogue. This kind of thoughtful timing shows that I care about her emotional state and strengthens the foundation of trust in our relationship.

Conversely, there are moments when we are both feeling particularly connected and engaged that might serve as an ideal backdrop for discussing important topics. For example, if Michelle and I are enjoying a quiet evening together, it might be a good time to discuss future goals or plans for our relationship. This allows both of us to approach the conversation with a clear mind and an open heart, introducing a constructive environment where ideas can flow freely, and both perspectives are valued.

Navigating Good Moments for Conversations

When it comes to determining the best time to converse, several factors can guide you. First, be attentive to each other's emotional states. If Michelle seems stressed, anxious, or distracted, she may not be in the right frame of mind for a deep conversation. Look for signs such as **body language**, **tone of voice**, or **willingness to engage**. Similarly, if you are feeling overwhelmed, it's important to recognize that your emotional state might inhibit a productive discussion.

Another hint for identifying good moments to talk is to create check-in routines. For example, dedicating Friday evenings to discussing your week and any upcoming challenges could provide a consistent, supportive time for both of you to share your thoughts. By establishing regular moments to connect, you reduce the pressure of having to bring up topics spontaneously and ensure that both of you are psychologically prepared for meaningful discussions.

Knowing When to Wait

It's just as important to know when to hold back on initiating a conversation. If you sense that a conversation could lead to conflict or hurt feelings, consider postponing it until emotions have cooled down or the environment is more favorable. For instance, if an issue arises during a family gathering or public setting, it's often best to table the discussion until you can talk privately. This not only protects your spouse's feelings but also maintains respect while demonstrating that you're committed to resolving the issue thoughtfully.

Pausing before broaching topics can be incredibly beneficial. For example, if you feel compelled to address a concern about behavior or expectations, take a moment to reflect on whether the timing is appropriate. By prioritizing good timing, you enhance the potential for constructive conversation that honors your relationship.

The effectiveness of conversations within a marriage is heavily influenced by timing. Michelle and I can cultivate our relationship by being mindful of each other's emotional readiness and by recognizing appropriate times to raise important topics. By being intentional in your communication habits and recognizing the signs of readiness, you create a safe space for ongoing dialogue, deepening both your understanding and connection as a couple.

Delivery

The delivery of your conversations plays a vital role in how effectively you communicate within your marriage. It is not just what you say, but how you say it that can either create intimacy and trust or create distance and misunderstanding. For Michelle and me, understanding the proper way to deliver a conversation is crucial for nurturing a strong relationship built on respect and love.

For example, imagine I need to discuss how to manage household responsibilities, a topic that can be sensitive. I approach Michelle after dinner when we both have had some time to unwind.

I say: *"Hey Hun, I really appreciate all that you do around the house. I wanted to talk about how we can better manage our chores together so they feel more balanced for both of us. How do you feel about that?"*

In this example, my delivery is thoughtful and respectful. By starting with appreciation, I acknowledge Michelle's efforts, which creates a sense of value. By framing the discussion as a collaborative effort and inviting her opinion, I promote intimacy and teamwork. This method of delivery creates a safe space for Michelle to share her thoughts openly and reduces the risk of defensiveness. The tone is gentle, inviting, and affirming, which encourages a constructive dialogue.

Now, consider a contrasting situation in which we approach the same topic with a different delivery.

I say: *"Michelle, can't you just handle your part of the chores for once? I'm tired of being the only one who's pulling weight around here!"*

In this scenario, my delivery is sharp and accusatory. By using a critical tone and making statements like "can't you just handle your part," I place blame, and it triggers defensiveness in Michelle. Such a delivery creates an environment of hostility and resentment rather than support and understanding. This approach not only diminishes the intimacy in our relationship but also risks escalating the conversation into a conflict rather than a constructive discussion.

The way you deliver your messages can either build trust or damage it. Respectful delivery involves being mindful of your tone, word choice, and body language. For instance, maintaining eye contact, using a calm voice, and avoiding aggressive gestures convey that you genuinely care about the conversation and your spouse's feelings. On the other hand, delivery that includes sarcasm, harshness, or blame can cause emotional wounds that may take time to heal.

By being intentional about how you choose to express your thoughts and feelings, you not only honor your spouse but also reinforce the bonds of your relationship.

Replacing Criticism with Curiosity

Criticism, particularly when it becomes a habitual pattern in a marriage, can be extremely detrimental to the relationship's health. It often leads to a breakdown in communication, erodes emotional intimacy, and creates an environment of defensiveness, which can ultimately contribute to marital dissatisfaction and conflict. According to research by John Gottman, a well-known relationship researcher, the use of criticism in a relationship is one of the "Four Horsemen" that predict divorce. His studies indicate that couples who frequently engage in criticism are significantly more likely to end in separation or divorce, as the perpetual feeling of being attacked can lead one partner to withdraw or retaliate rather than nurture a constructive dialogue.

Moreover, the psychological impact of criticism shouldn't be underestimated. Constantly facing criticism can lead to increased stress, lowered self-esteem, and a sense of inadequacy for the individual on the receiving end. A study conducted by the Journal of Marriage and Family revealed that critical communication often correlates with depressive symptoms and overall dissatisfaction within the marriage. This toxicity can create a vicious cycle where one partner's criticism invites defensiveness from the other, perpetuating a hostile atmosphere that further entrenches misunderstandings and conflict. Recognizing and addressing critical communication patterns is essential for couples to build a healthy, supportive, and loving relationship, emphasizing constructive feedback rather than harmful critique.

Criticism versus complaining

In a marriage, the distinction between complaining and criticizing is crucial for maintaining a healthy relationship. Complaining can be a legitimate way to express feelings and frustrations about specific behaviors or situations, whereas criticism involves attacking a partner's character or intentions. For instance, let's consider Michelle and me. If I say, *"I feel overwhelmed when dishes are left in the sink,"* this is a complaint. It expresses my feelings and focuses on a specific behavior that needs to be addressed. On the other hand, if I say, *"You never care about keeping the house clean,"* it shifts into criticism, attacking Michelle's character and implying a flaw in who she is rather than pointing out a behavior.

To encourage a constructive dialogue, couples need to avoid accusatory language and negative absolutes such as "never" or "always," as these words can escalate tensions and trigger defensiveness. For example, instead of saying, *"You always forget to take out the trash,"* which places blame and generates a counterproductive atmosphere, you might say, *"I get anxious when the trash isn't taken out on schedule."* This approach can lead to a more open and workable conversation. Research has shown that constructive complaints, those that convey feelings without blame, are more likely to lead to positive resolutions and to enhance emotional intimacy. The work of John Gottman points out that couples who regularly engage in positive rather than negative communication are significantly happier and more stable in their marriages.

Using the words "never" or "always" in a critical way during conversations often misrepresents a partner's behavior. For example, statements like *"You never help with the chores"* or *"You always forget to call me"* imply an absolute and unchanging quality about the partner's actions. However, such generalizations tend to overlook exceptions and nuances in behavior, leading to an inaccurate portrayal of the individual and their contributions to the relationship.

Complain vs Criticize

TRAIT	COMPLAIN	CRITICIZE
Definition	Express dissatisfaction or annoyance about something	Express disapproval or find fault with something
Tone	Can be more emotional or personal	Usually more objective or analytical
Intent	To voice grievances or seek resolution	To point out flaws or shortcomings
Impact	Can lead to change or improvements	May cause resentment or defensiveness

By declaring that someone "never" or "always" does something, it not only exaggerates the situation but also diminishes the person's previous positive behaviors or efforts. In reality, most individuals will have moments when they fulfill and neglect certain responsibilities. When addressing a specific concern, it is more constructive to point out instances that you find challenging, as this approach acknowledges the complexity of human behavior and avoids casting the partner in a negative, unchanging light. For instance, instead of saying *"You never help with dinner,"* one might say, *"I've noticed you haven't helped with dinner this week, which has been tough for me."* This way, the focus is on the behavior rather than labeling the whole person, thereby reducing defensiveness and cultivating a more productive conversation. Avoiding absolutes like "never" or "always" enhances communication and supports a more supportive dialogue, thereby facilitating understanding and collaboration within the relationship.

A shift in language, from critical accusations to the expression of specific feelings and needs, can prevent misunderstandings and encourage collaboration in problem-solving. Studies suggest that addressing grievances constructively can significantly improve relationship satisfaction and reduce the likelihood of conflict escalation. By striving to express ourselves thoughtfully and compassionately, you can cultivate a partnership rooted in trust and support rather than discord.

Another surefire way to address the criticizing talk is to replace it with curiosity. Replacing criticism in conversations with curiosity is a powerful strategy that can transform the way partners communicate, promoting understanding and connection rather than defensiveness and conflict. When we approach a situation with genuine curiosity, we shift from a mindset of judgment and blame to one of inquiry and understanding. This change in perspective encourages a more open and constructive dialogue.

For example, let's say I notice that Michelle has been late to several of the meetups we've planned together. Instead of expressing frustration with a critical statement like, *"You always keep me waiting and never respect my time,"* I might approach the situation with curiosity by saying, *"I'm curious. I've noticed you've been late a few times recently. Is there something going on that's making it hard for you to arrive on time?"* This inquisitive approach invites Michelle to share her perspective and challenges, while acknowledging my frustration without making her feel attacked. It opens the door for a supportive conversation about what might be causing the delays and how we can work together to improve the situation.

Additionally, curiosity can extend beyond specific behaviors to encompass your partner's broader emotional landscape. If Michelle expresses sadness or frustration, instead of resorting to criticism by saying, *"You're always in a bad mood lately,"* I could ask, *"I'm curious, I've noticed you seem a bit down. Can we talk about what's been on your mind?"* Demonstrating genuine curiosity not only helps to clarify intentions and feelings but also strengthens emotional intimacy, as it shows your partner that you care about their experiences and are interested in listening to them.

Research in communication and relationship dynamics supports the effectiveness of this approach. John Gottman emphasizes that curiosity in conversations can be a form of emotional intelligence that enhances the likelihood of resolving conflicts and building deeper connections. By nurturing a habit of approaching your partner with questions rather than accusations, you create an environment where both partners feel respected, understood, and valued. This shift from criticism to curiosity can lead to healthier, more satisfying partnerships, where open dialogue replaces defensiveness, ultimately contributing to a happier marriage.

How to Avoid Harsh, Sarcastic, or Dismissive Talk

Harsh, sarcastic, and dismissive talk can be incredibly destructive to maintaining a positive atmosphere in a relationship. Such communication styles often convey contempt, suggesting that one partner does not value the other's thoughts or feelings. For instance, responding to a spouse's concerns with sarcasm like saying, *"Oh sure, because that's all I want to hear right now!"*, invalidates their feelings and can cause significant emotional harm. Harsh words easily escalate conflicts, shifting the conversation from addressing a problem to a defensive battle where both partners may feel demeaned or disrespected. Research by John Gottman reveals that contempt is one of the strongest predictors of relationship breakdown, highlighting the destructive nature of such communication.

Adopting a constructive approach to communication can significantly reduce the occurrences of harsh, sarcastic, or dismissive talk. One way to avoid this is by practicing active listening, which involves genuinely engaging with your partner's thoughts and feelings without judgment. For example, if Michelle shares her frustration about a challenging day, instead of responding dismissively, I might say, *"I'm sorry to hear that. Can you tell me more about what's been bothering you?"* This response not only shows that I value her feelings but also encourages an open dialogue where she feels heard and supported.

It's essential to cultivate a language of respect and support in your conversations. When you feel the urge to be sarcastic or dismissive, take a moment to pause and reflect on how you can express your thoughts constructively. For instance, expressing your feelings without attacking your partner might look like, *"I feel overwhelmed by this situation, and I'd appreciate your help,"* instead of saying, *"You never understand how hard this is for me."* By focusing on "I" statements, you take ownership of your feelings and promote a collaborative atmosphere. Practicing these strategies can create a nurturing environment that cultivates emotional intimacy and strengthens the relationship over time. When you think about the different ways we can respond in a bad way, remember, we wouldn't want to be talked to like that either. The golden rule definitely applies here!

Communicating Truth in a Way that Builds Up, Not Tears Down

In all conversations, especially within the context of a marriage, it is essential to communicate truth in a manner that builds up rather than tears down. The Bible provides clear guidance on this principle, especially in verses like Ephesians 4:29, which states, *"Do not let any unwholesome talk come out of your mouths, but only what is helpful for building others up according to their needs, that it may benefit those who listen."* This scripture reinforces the importance of mindful communication that seeks to uplift and support one another, rather than damaging the relational fabric with harsh or unkind words.

Our words have a unique ability to reflect our inner character and who we truly are. In Matthew 12:34, Jesus says, *"For out of the abundance of the heart the mouth speaks."* This insight emphasizes that the way we communicate reveals the true state of our hearts.

When we speak with kindness, consideration, and love, we reflect the character of Christ within us. Conversely, when we resort to criticism, sarcasm, or dismissive language, we may reveal anger, frustration, or bitterness, harming our relationships and portraying a negative image of ourselves as followers of Christ.

To embody biblical principles in our communication, we should strive to follow the guidance of Colossians 4:6, which encourages us to *"Let your conversation be always full of grace, seasoned with salt, so that you may know how to answer everyone."* This verse suggests that our speech should not only convey truth but also be marked by grace, creating an environment where each person feels valued and respected. By intentionally aligning our words with biblical truths that emphasize building others up, we not only nurture healthier relationships but also embody the love and grace of Christ in our interactions, creating a positive atmosphere in our marriages and families.

As we wrap up our chapter on the power of communication, it's clear that choosing our words wisely is essential to a thriving relationship. After all, it's not just about what we say, but how we say it. Much like your favorite coffee order, communication should be tailored, strong enough to get the point across but sweetened with a bit of kindness to make it palatable! Remember, using harsh words can lead to some bitter brews, while a sprinkle of curiosity and a dash of grace can turn any conversation into a warm, inviting exchange.

As we venture forward, let's commit to building each other up with our words, avoiding the "never" and "always" traps, and trading criticism for curiosity. Because no matter how frustrating the toaster can be, trust me, we've all had those mornings, it's worth remembering that our goal is connection, not contention.

Chapter Four

Understanding Your Spouse's Communication Style

Biblical Foundation: Romans 12:6, 1 Peter 3:7

Men are from Mars and Women are from Venus. When I saw that book on a shelf once, I thought, "How True!" Of course, when I had that thought, I was replaying a joke in my head about how men never understand women! But it wasn't until I was married that that reality showed itself to be true in so many ways! One of those ways is the way we communicate. In order to have a flourishing marriage, we must understand our spouse's communication style, a crucial key to unlocking the door of effective dialogue and deeper connection in your marriage. Just as God created each of us as unique individuals (with our own quirks and oddities), He also gave us different ways to express our thoughts and feelings. Some of us may be straightforward like a power tool, while others might communicate more like an intricate timepiece, with gears that take some time to understand.

When it comes to communication, it's essential to recognize that your spouse's style isn't a puzzle to be solved, but a beautiful masterpiece waiting to be explored. Think of it this way: in the grand orchestra of marriage, your partner may play the violin while you're on the drums. The goal isn't for one to take the lead and drown out the other, but rather to harmonize, creating a rich melody together. So, as we dive into this chapter, let's unpack those unique styles, because understanding your spouse's way of communicating may save your marriage from a "misunderstanding" scene worthy of a sitcom!

The Four Primary Communication Styles (Expressive, Analytical, Assertive, Nurturing)

In this chapter, we will explore the four primary communication styles that significantly influence how we interact with our spouses: **expressive**, **analytical**, **assertive**, and **nurturing**. Each style has unique characteristics and communication approaches that can either facilitate understanding or create confusion in relationships. By recognizing and appreciating these differences, we can improve our interactions and create deeper connections with our partners.

1. Expressive: The expressive communicator thrives on sharing emotions and thoughts openly. They often use vivid language, storytelling, and emotional appeals to convey their messages. This style is characterized by enthusiasm and spontaneity, making expressive communicators engaging conversationalists. However, their emotional intensity can sometimes overwhelm more reserved partners, leading to misunderstandings if not balanced with active listening.

2. Analytical: Analytical communicators prioritize logic, details, and rationality in conversations. They tend to process information thoroughly before expressing their thoughts, often relying on data and factual evidence to support their points. While analytical communicators can provide clarity and structure in discussions, they may come across as detached or overly critical, especially to more feeling-oriented partners who seek emotional connection.

3. Assertive: Assertive communicators possess a balanced blend of confidence and respect. They express their thoughts and feelings clearly, without being aggressive or passive. This style is characterized by directness and certainty, allowing assertive communicators to advocate for their needs while still valuing others' perspectives. However, they need to be mindful of their tone to avoid appearing confrontational.

4. Nurturing: Nurturing communicators are empathetic and focused on building rapport and emotional security in conversations. They prioritize feelings and connections, often seeking to deeply understand their partner's emotions and needs. This style encourages a warm, supportive environment, but it can sometimes lead to avoiding difficult topics or to direct confrontation, as nurturers may prioritize harmony over honesty in challenging discussions.

As we break down these styles, we'll explore how understanding each one can enhance communication, reduce conflict, and strengthen your marriage. By appreciating the strengths and weaknesses of our spouses' communication styles, we can engage more effectively and cultivate a harmonious relationship.

First, let's look at the expressive communicator.

Imagine a scenario in which an expressive communicator, Sarah, feels overwhelmed by her workload at home and needs to voice her frustrations to her spouse, John. Sarah enters the living room, her emotions bubbling over, and she begins her expression like this:

John, I just need to talk to you for a minute! I feel like I'm drowning in chores and responsibilities. I mean, I'm trying to manage everything, between work, the kids' schedules, and house duties. Sometimes it feels like no one notices how much I'm doing! It's exhausting, and I just need someone to hear me! I feel like I'm on the verge of a meltdown!

In this response, Sarah uses her expressive communication style to convey not only her frustrations but also the emotional weight she carries. Her words are vivid and passionate, reflecting her need for validation and acknowledgment of her struggles.

When addressing an expressive communicator like Sarah, it's crucial to respond with empathy and acknowledgment. John could reply in the following way:

Sarah, I really hear you. It sounds like you're feeling really overwhelmed, and I can see how hard you're working to juggle everything. I appreciate everything you do for us, and it's important for me to understand what you're feeling. Let's take a moment to discuss how we can better share the load. What can I do to support you right now?

In this response, John effectively validates Sarah's feelings by using active listening skills and expressing empathy. Key elements include:

1. Acknowledgment: By saying, "I hear you," John reassures Sarah that her feelings are being recognized.

2. Empathy: He articulates an understanding of her situation, affirming that her emotions are valid.

3. Supportive Action: John's offer to discuss how to support her not only conveys that he cares but also opens the door for collaborative problem-solving, which can relieve some pressure from Sarah.

This type of response helps Sarah feel seen and understood, creating a safe environment where she can express herself without fear of dismissal. It strengthens communication and connection between them, enabling them to work together effectively toward solutions.

Secondly, let's look at the analytical communicator.

Mark and Lisa own a business that they operate together. Let's consider a scenario where an analytical communicator, Mark, is experiencing frustration with a team project at work. He feels the project plan lacks clear data and objectives, which is causing confusion among team members. Mark decides to address this issue during a meeting with his spouse, Lisa.

Lisa, I need to discuss something that's been bothering me. I was reviewing the project outline and realized the objectives are not sufficiently defined. For instance, the goals outlined in Section 2 are vague and lack measurable criteria. We need to clarify these benchmarks if we want the team to stay on track. Based on my calculations, if we don't set these parameters, we risk falling behind the project timeline by approximately 15%. This could impact not only the team's performance but also our client's expectations.

In this example, Mark uses his analytical communication style to share his concerns. He's focused on data, logical reasoning, and specific details, which clearly convey his frustration about the project's ambiguity.

To show she genuinely understands Mark's concerns, Lisa should respond in a way that acknowledges his perspective while maintaining the logical approach he appreciates. A suitable response might be:

Mark, I see where you're coming from. It sounds like the lack of clear objectives is adding unnecessary pressure on you and the team. I appreciate how you've broken down the issue with specific data, especially the impact on the timeline. What do you think we can do to clarify those objectives? Perhaps we can outline the measurable criteria together to ensure the team has a clear path forward?

In this response, Lisa effectively validates Mark's analytical approach with the following key elements:

1. Acknowledgment: By acknowledging his concerns and reiterating his logical points, Lisa shows that she understands the importance of clarity and structure in the project.

2. Validation of Data: Referring to Mark's calculations reinforces that she appreciates his analysis and expertise, ensuring he feels his input is valued.

3. Collaborative Problem-Solving: By asking for Mark's thoughts on how to address the issue, Lisa builds a collaborative atmosphere where his analytical skills can contribute to a solution.

This type of response creates a sense of understanding for Mark, allowing him to feel validated in his logical approach. It introduces a productive dialogue in which both partners can engage fully, enabling them to address issues effectively.

Third, let's look at the assertive communication style.

Let's look at an assertive communicator, Jenna, who is experiencing conflicts at work with her colleagues over project responsibilities. She's noticed that some tasks are being neglected, which could affect their deadlines. Jenna decides to bring this up with her spouse, Tom, to clearly express her thoughts.

Tom, I want to talk about something that's been on my mind. I've noticed that during our project meetings, there's confusion about who is responsible for certain tasks. I value teamwork, and I think it's essential that we clarify everyone's roles to ensure we meet our deadlines. I believe that a clearer division of responsibilities will lead to better collaboration and less stress for all of us.

In this scenario, Jenna uses her assertive communication style to address the issue confidently and respectfully. She expresses her feelings and provides clear observations, making her needs known without being aggressive.

To validate Jenna's assertive communication style, Tom should respond with acknowledgment and openness, reinforcing her confidence while also inviting further conversation. A suitable response might be:

Jenna, I appreciate you bringing this up. It sounds like you've identified an important issue, and I completely agree that clarifying roles would make a huge difference for the team. I'm glad to hear you're addressing it directly; let's brainstorm together on how you can facilitate that conversation in your next team meeting. What do you think would be the best approach?

In this response, Tom effectively supports Jenna's assertive communication with several key components:

1. Acknowledgment: By saying "I appreciate you bringing this up," Tom shows that he values her initiative and feels comfortable addressing challenges.

2. Validation: He recognizes Jenna's observations and emphasizes their importance, reinforcing her perspective.

3. Collaborative and Proactive: By suggesting they brainstorm together, Tom invites Jenna to not only lead the conversation but also to involve himself in seeking solutions, demonstrating his support for her assertiveness.

By responding in this manner, Tom helps Jenna feel understood and respected, reinforcing her confidence as an assertive communicator. This open exchange creates an environment where both partners can discuss issues constructively and encourage one another as they navigate challenges together.

Let's now look at the nurturing communication style.

Let's examine a scenario in which a nurturing communicator, Emily, is feeling distressed about the emotional climate in her friend group. She has noticed rising tensions and unresolved conflicts that are causing friends to feel distant from one another. Emily decides to discuss her feelings with her spouse, Alex, in hopes of finding a supportive way to approach the situation.

Alex, I've been feeling really concerned about our friends lately. It seems like there's a lot of unspoken tension during our get-togethers, and it makes me sad to see everyone feeling so disconnected. I just want to ensure that everyone feels valued and supported. I think we should check in with them individually to see how they're feeling. It's important to me that we create a warm and caring environment where everyone can express their emotions openly.

In this example, Emily uses her nurturing communication style to articulate her concerns and desires. Her focus is on her friends' emotional well-being and the need for a connected, supportive atmosphere.

To validate Emily's nurturing communication style, Alex should respond with warmth and encouragement, reinforcing her feelings while also engaging with her concerns. A suitable response might be:

Emily, I really appreciate you sharing these thoughts with me. It's clear how much you care about our friends and their well-being. I agree that creating a supportive environment is important, and I love your idea of checking in with them. Let's make a plan together on how we can reach out, perhaps over coffee or dinner. It's important to me too that everyone feels valued and heard.

In this response, Alex effectively supports Emily's nurturing communication with several key elements:

1. Acknowledgment: By expressing appreciation for Emily's concern, Alex shows that he values her feelings and recognizes the importance she places on relationships.

2. Validation of Emotions: By agreeing with Emily's perspective, he reinforces her emotional concerns and emphasizes that her desires are important.

3. Collaborative and Supportive Action: By suggesting a plan to reach out to their friends together, Alex affirms his commitment to the relationship while also engaging with Emily's nurturing nature.

This type of response encourages a sense of understanding and support for Emily, helping her feel validated in her caring approach. It creates a safe environment for both partners to discuss feelings openly, encouraging collaboration and reinforcing their emotional connection.

Understanding each spouse's communication style is crucial to promoting effective communication in a marriage. Each style has distinct characteristics and preferences that impact how messages are conveyed, interpreted, and understood. Recognizing these unique needs facilitates clear communication as expressive individuals typically seek emotional connection, analytical types crave logic, assertive communicators value directness, and nurturing partners prioritize empathy. By acknowledging and valuing diverse communication styles, couples promote empathy and respect, which are essential for a healthy relationship. This awareness helps prevent dismissive comments and encourages patience, especially when one spouse feels their partner is "overthinking."

Additionally, understanding each other's styles enhances conflict resolution; different styles approach conflict in varying ways, allowing couples to tailor their strategies for resolving disputes and reducing misinterpretations. This understanding also improves collaboration, enabling partners to leverage each other's strengths, such as an analytical spouse excelling at problem-solving while an expressive partner helps convey messages in a more relatable manner. By being sensitive to each other's communication styles, spouses can provide appropriate support, creating opportunities for deeper connections and trust. Such awareness nurtures an atmosphere where partners feel safe to express differing opinions, encouraging open dialogue and ultimately leading to personal growth as individuals adapt and integrate traits from each other's styles. As couples navigate conflicts and build intimacy, they establish a foundation of mutual understanding and respect, vital to a thriving partnership.

How Upbringing, Culture, and Past Wounds Shape Communication

A person's communication style is significantly influenced by their upbringing, cultural background, and past wounds, all of which shape how they express themselves and interpret others' messages. **Upbringing** plays a pivotal role in establishing foundational communication patterns, with family dynamics and parental models serving as examples from which individuals learn to communicate. **Cultural factors** also contribute, as different cultures emphasize different values, such as directness, emotional expression, or group harmony, which impact how individuals share thoughts and feelings. **Past wounds**, such as experiences of trauma or neglect, can create barriers to open communication or instigate defensiveness, leading individuals to develop coping mechanisms that influence their interactions. As we examine these interconnected factors, we can better understand the complexities of communication styles and the hidden challenges couples may face in their relationships.

Upbringing

Upbringing plays a formative role in shaping an individual's communication style, significantly influencing how they interact with their spouse in marriage. The communication dynamics observed in childhood, particularly between parents and caregivers, serve as prototypes for future interactions. Children absorb language, behavioral patterns, conflict resolution strategies, and emotional responses by observing their parents' communication styles. This foundational experience can lead to the incorporation of both positive and negative habits into adult relationships.

For instance, if a child witnesses open communication, constructive dialogue, and emotional expression in their family, they are more likely to adopt similar practices in their marriage. Studies indicate that children from families where effective communication is modeled tend to develop healthier relational skills, such as empathy and active listening. According to research published by the American Psychological Association, effective communication within the family is correlated with higher levels of marital satisfaction later in life, as patterns established in childhood tend to carry over into adult relationships.

Conversely, if a child grows up in a home where communication is frequently negative, dismissive, or conflict-avoidant, they may inherit detrimental habits that negatively impact their marriage. For example, a child exposed to parental arguments or silence may struggle with openness, conflict resolution, and emotional expression as an adult. A study published in the Journal of Marriage and Family found that children who experienced high levels of household conflict were more likely to experience difficulties in their adult relationships, including higher rates of dissatisfaction and a tendency to engage in conflict rather than resolve it.

Additionally, the phenomenon of "intergenerational transmission" explains how communication styles and relational patterns are passed down through generations. Studies in family psychology show that individuals tend to recreate dynamics similar to those in their childhood relationships. For example, those raised in environments where affection was scarce or criticism was prevalent may struggle to express warmth or default to critical patterns, potentially leading to cycles of misunderstanding and conflict in their marriages.

A deep understanding of one's upbringing, including parental models, is vital for understanding one's communication style in marriage. By recognizing the good and bad habits learned from past experiences, couples can seek to change negative communication patterns and encourage healthier interactions. This awareness not only promotes individual growth but can also enhance the overall quality of the marital relationship, leading to a more nurturing and effective partnership. Couples equipped with this knowledge can engage in targeted communication strategies that break negative cycles and build a more harmonious future together.

Culture

A person's cultural background and traits significantly shape their communication style, influencing how they interact within their marriage and how they relate to their spouse. Culture encompasses shared beliefs, values, customs, and social practices that shape behavior and communication, deeply informing how individuals express feelings, resolve disagreements, and engage in intimacy. These cultural factors can lead to the adoption of both beneficial and detrimental communication habits that affect marital dynamics.

One crucial aspect of cultural influence is the distinction between individualism and collectivism. In individualistic cultures, such as those often found in Western societies, communication tends to be more direct and assertive. Individuals are encouraged to express their opinions, assert their needs, and engage in open confrontation. Consequently, partners from these backgrounds may approach conflict resolution with a focus on addressing issues directly and valuing personal expression. Research published in the journal Communication Research shows that individuals from individualistic cultures generally exhibit higher levels of self-disclosure, which is essential for building intimacy in relationships and may lead to healthier communication in marriages.

Conversely, collectivist cultures, predominantly found in many Asian, African, and Latin American societies, tend to emphasize group harmony and the needs of the family or community over individual desires. In these contexts, communication may be more indirect, with an emphasis on non-verbal cues, implicit messages, and maintaining harmony to avoid conflict. Partners from collectivist cultures may prioritize relational dynamics over direct confrontations, sometimes leading to unresolved issues or a lack of open discussion about personal feelings. A study by Morley and McGlone found that individuals from collectivist cultures often use avoidance or accommodation strategies when faced with conflict, which can create challenges in marriage, as issues may be swept under the rug rather than addressed.

Additionally, the cultural dimension of power distance, how different cultures perceive and handle power inequalities, also influences communication. In cultures with high power distance, such as certain Asian and Middle Eastern countries, communication often reflects hierarchical relationships, leading individuals to defer to authority or to be less assertive in expressing their thoughts. This deferential communication can carry over into marriage, shaping how decisions are made and how couples express disagreement. A study by Hofstede found that high power distance is associated with lower marital communication satisfaction, as individuals may feel unable to voice their opinions due to ingrained power dynamics in their cultural background.

Cultural narratives surrounding gender roles further shape communication styles within marriage. Many cultures carry distinct expectations about how males and females should communicate. For instance, in cultures with traditional gender roles, men might be socialized to communicate in more assertive or authoritative ways. At the same time, women may be taught to be more nurturing and indirect. This can lead to communication complications when expectations clash, resulting in misunderstandings. A notable study from the Journal of Marriage and Family found that traditional gender role socialization often leads to dissatisfaction in communication between partners, as men and women may struggle to align their communication styles and needs.

Marriage across cultural backgrounds can create both opportunities and challenges. Couples who are aware of their cultural influences can leverage their diverse communication styles to enrich their relationship. For example, the assertiveness found in individualistic cultures may balance the relational sensitivity of collectivist backgrounds, resulting in a more integrated approach to communication. A study published in the European Journal of Communication found that intercultural couples who actively discuss their cultural differences tend to report greater communication satisfaction and lower levels of conflict.

A person's cultural background and traits deeply influence their communication style, carrying both good and bad habits into their marital relationships. Understanding how individual backgrounds inform communication can empower couples to recognize and address potential barriers, generating healthier interactions and ultimately leading to more fulfilling marriages. By developing cultural competence and employing open dialogue about their communication styles, couples can navigate cultural differences more effectively, creating a partnership that respects both individual and shared backgrounds while enriching their emotional connection.

Past Wounds

A person's past wounds and trauma from previous relationships can significantly influence their communication style in their current marriage, impacting how they interact with their spouse and how they manage conflict, intimacy, and emotional expression. Experience shapes behavior, and unresolved emotional issues can lead to the projection of past relationship dynamics onto new partnerships, often with detrimental effects.

For many, past wounds manifest as communication barriers during conflict or discussions of sensitive topics. Individuals who have experienced trauma, such as emotional abuse, neglect, or betrayal, may develop specific coping mechanisms that affect their communication styles. For instance, those who have faced emotional neglect may struggle to articulate their needs or feelings, leading to frustration and misunderstandings in their current relationships. A study published in the journal Emotion found that individuals with a history of attachment-related trauma often exhibit heightened anxiety and defensiveness during discussions, making it challenging for them to engage in open, vulnerable dialogue with their partners.

Another common effect of past relationship trauma is the tendency towards avoidance or withdrawal during conflicts. Individuals who have experienced volatile or harmful interactions in previous relationships may be wary of confrontation and therefore resort to silence or evasion when faced with disagreements. This conflict avoidance can inadvertently escalate issues, as unresolved problems tend to grow over time due to a lack of communication. Research published in the Journal of Marriage and Family found that couples who employ avoidance strategies were more likely to report high levels of dissatisfaction and lower levels of commitment, as fundamental issues remained unaddressed and contributed to emotional distance.

In contrast, some individuals may become overly confrontational, mirroring the aggressive dynamics of previous relationships. This behavior can stem from a need to regain control or assert themselves, particularly if they felt powerless in past situations. Studies indicate that aggressive communication patterns often lead to escalating conflicts instead of resolution, causing emotional distress for both partners. A meta-analysis in the Psychological Bulletin revealed that aggressive communication was a significant predictor of relationship dissatisfaction and even divorce, as partners may feel attacked rather than supported.

Furthermore, past experiences can impact the vulnerability required for healthy communication. Individuals who have been betrayed or deeply hurt may find it difficult to trust their partners fully. This can lead to a reluctance to open up, share feelings, or express affection, which is vital for nurturing an emotional connection in marriage. According to research published in The Journal of Social Issues, those who have experienced relational traumas may exhibit a fear of intimacy, leading to difficulties in creating deep emotional bonds with their spouses. This fear can manifest in various ways, such as avoiding discussions about future plans or reluctance to show affection, creating barriers to effective communication.

The phenomenon of "relationship anxiety" also emerges from past traumas. Individuals may feel a persistent fear that their partner will leave them or that they will repeat past mistakes. This anxiety can lead to communication habits characterized by panic or over-analysis during interactions, further complicating marital discourse. A study published in Personal Relationships found that relationship anxiety was linked to negative communication patterns, such as excessive questioning or a need for reassurance, which can overwhelm partners and strain relationships.

It's important to note that while past wounds can present significant challenges, they can also motivate individuals to seek healing and nurture positive communication habits. Many people learn valuable lessons from their experiences, leading them to be more empathetic or to become more aware of communication patterns that elicit conflict. For instance, someone who has experienced emotional neglect may be more inclined to express appreciation for their partner's efforts, thereby encouraging a more positive communication environment.

Couples therapy or relationship counseling can be particularly beneficial for navigating the complexities of past wounds, allowing partners to develop healthier communication strategies. Research by the American Association for Marriage and Family Therapy highlights that couples participating in therapy often report improved communication skills and a greater ability to express emotions constructively.

Past wounds and trauma from previous relationships profoundly shape communication styles in current marriages, influencing how individuals express themselves and engage with their partners. Understanding these dynamics can help couples recognize patterns, address barriers, and cultivate healthier communication habits. By acknowledging the impact of past experiences, individuals can work towards healing and building a stronger, more responsive marital relationship that prioritizes open dialogue, empathy, and mutual understanding.

Recognizing and Respecting Personality Differences

Understanding the different personalities of spouses is essential to maintaining healthy, fruitful marriages. God's design in creating different personalities enriches our relationships and presents opportunities for growth, balance, and mutual respect. Our differences can become strengths rather than points of contention, highlighting how uniquely we reflect God's creation.

The biblical foundation for this understanding is rooted in Genesis 1:27, which states, *"So God created mankind in his own image; in the image of God, he created them; male and female he created them."* This verse demonstrates the inherent diversity in creation, signifying that each individual, shaped by distinct traits and personalities, brings a unique perspective. Additionally, in 1 Corinthians 12:12-14, Paul discusses the diversity of the body of Christ, emphasizing that different parts perform unique functions. This analogy can be applied to marriage, where differing personalities contribute to a more dynamic and robust partnership.

Research in psychology supports the idea that distinct personality types significantly affect relationship dynamics. For instance, the Myers-Briggs Type Indicator (MBTI) categorizes personalities based on how individuals interact with the world, often revealing that opposites tend to attract, as differing traits can complement one another. According to a survey conducted by the American Psychological Association, couples who embrace and celebrate their differences report higher levels of satisfaction compared to those who share too many similar traits. Furthermore, when spouses possess very similar personalities, they may find themselves clashing over approaches to life and problem-solving. For example, two highly extroverted partners might struggle to negotiate social plans and clash over the need for downtime. Thus, too much similarity can lead to stagnation and an echo chamber of thought.

Recognizing and respecting these differences is vital for a healthy marriage. Acknowledging that each spouse brings unique strengths can help shape discussions about challenges. When disagreements arise, they can be seen as opportunities to appreciate each partner's diverse perspectives rather than as threats to the relationship. Cultivating a culture of respect involves effective communication and valuing each other's viewpoints. Using "I" statements can help partners express their feelings without placing blame, ensuring both feel heard and respected.

Personality differences can be transformed into strengths. Often, the strengths of one partner can compensate for the weaknesses of another; for instance, a detail-oriented spouse may help ground the spontaneity of a more free-spirited partner. This balance can lead to well-rounded decision-making and enhanced problem-solving. Embracing diverse personalities encourages teamwork and collaboration. Implementing strategies that leverage each spouse's strengths, for example, budgeting together, with one focusing on details and the other on broader planning, can create unity within the relationship.

In our marriage, my realist approach often contrasts with Michelle's buoyant optimism, creating a dynamic that requires careful navigation. As a realist, I tend to analyze situations through a lens of practicality and caution, focusing on potential challenges and realities that need to be addressed. For instance, when planning a project or deciding on a family vacation, I naturally consider all possible obstacles, from budgeting constraints to logistical hurdles. While I believe this helps with preparation, my tendency to focus on "what could go wrong" risks being perceived as negative or discouraging, particularly when Michelle's enthusiasm shines with ideas and possibilities. Her optimistic outlook energizes discussions, typically envisioning joyful outcomes and exciting experiences. This inherent positivity brings a refreshing perspective, reminding us to enjoy life and embrace potential joy in every situation.

However, these differing views can also lead to misunderstandings if not managed well. Michelle may feel that my focus on realism dampens her excitement, while I might think that her unfettered optimism overlooks practical realities. To make the most of our differences, we recognize the need for open communication and mutual respect. We strive to create an environment where each viewpoint is valued; I call attention to important details while Michelle encourages creativity and hope. By doing so, we not only avoid unnecessary conflict but also enrich our decision-making process. Together, we can blend my cautious approach with her optimistic vision, turning what initially seems like discord into a powerful unity that enhances our relationship and strengthens our bond. This conscious accommodation of our different perspectives ultimately cultivates a deeper appreciation for each other's strengths and encourages a more harmonious partnership.

Celebrating the differences inherent in God's intentional design helps couples build stronger, more resilient marriages. By recognizing, respecting, and utilizing each other's unique personalities, spouses can learn from one another, grow together, and fulfill God's purpose for their union. It is essential to view these differences as gifts rather than sources of friction. By nurturing them with understanding, love, and respect, couples can cultivate a thriving marriage that beautifully reflects God's creation.

Ultimately, creating an open dialogue about each other's personalities encourages deeper understanding and appreciation. Utilizing personality assessments can facilitate this understanding, and regularly expressing gratitude for each partner's distinct qualities can enhance relational satisfaction. By approaching marriage with the mindset that our different personalities can lead to growth and strength, couples can enjoy a fulfilling and meaningful partnership.

What Your Spouse Needs to Feel Understood and Valued

Understanding the distinct communication needs of men and women can significantly enhance marital harmony, reflecting God's intention for relationships.

3 TOP COMMUNICATION NEEDS

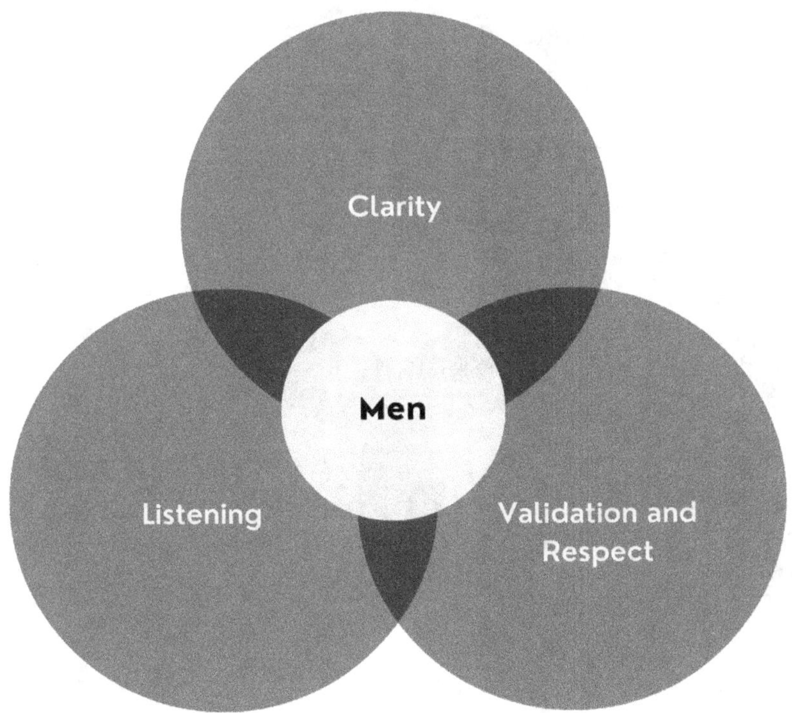

The top three communication needs for men often include:

- **Clarity:** Men typically appreciate straightforward and direct communication, which helps eliminate ambiguity and misunderstandings.

- **Listening:** They want to feel that their words are truly heard, which creates a sense of connection and significance.

- **Validation and respect:** Men seek acknowledgment of their feelings and thoughts, reinforcing their worth and contributing to their emotional security.

3 TOP COMMUNICATION NEEDS

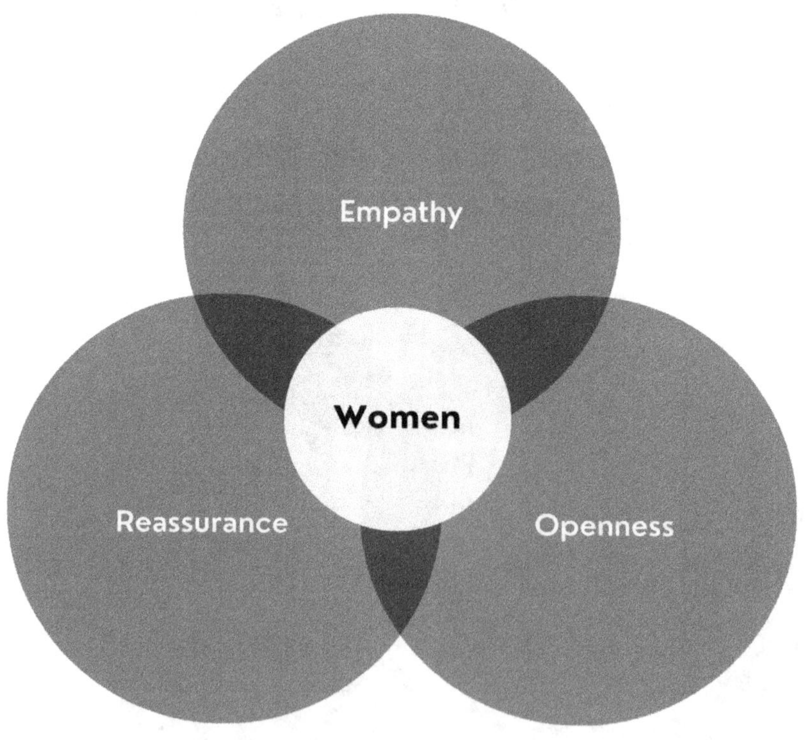

In contrast, the top three communication needs for women often encompass:

- **Empathy:** Women often look for emotional connection and understanding, desiring their partners to sympathize with their experiences and feelings.

- **Reassurance:** They frequently need verbal affirmations of love, support, and commitment, which help to solidify their sense of security in the relationship.

- **Openness:** Women desire open dialogues, where they can express feelings freely and engage in discussions without fear of judgment or dismissal.

In cultivating a healthy and loving marriage, spouses must prioritize mutual understanding and fulfillment of these communication needs. When both partners feel respected, acknowledged, and connected, one through clarity and validation, the others through empathy and reassurance, it strengthens their bond. It develops an environment of love and harmony. This divine design for relationships reminds us of God's intention as captured in Ephesians 4:2-3, where we are encouraged to bear with one another in love, creating a space where both spouses flourish emotionally and spiritually. By actively addressing and valuing each other's communication needs, couples can cultivate a deeper love that reflects God's character and design for marital unity.

Feeling understood and valued is foundational to a thriving marital relationship, functioning much like a "love tank" that, when full, nurtures intimacy and connection between spouses. When one partner experiences empathy and is genuinely heard, it satisfies their emotional needs, creating a sense of safety and acceptance. This understanding reassures them that their feelings, thoughts, and perspectives matter, effectively validating their existence within the relationship.

When each spouse prioritizes the other's emotional needs, a reciprocal dynamic is created. For instance, when a husband feels respected and validated in his opinions and experiences, he is more likely to reciprocate by listening to his wife and providing reassurance. This mutual exchange cultivates deeper emotional intimacy, facilitating a bond that encompasses trust and vulnerability.

Remember, God designed marriage as a partnership in which both spouses reflect Christ's love for the church (Ephesians 5:25). Therefore, honoring and valuing one another is a manifestation of divine love, in which each partner actively seeks to uplift the other. As couples fill each other's love tanks through intentional actions, such as validating feelings or offering heartfelt encouragement, they cultivate a stronger sense of unity. This not only nurtures a deeper connection but also allows spouses to support one another in personal growth, ultimately leading to a harmonious, flourishing relationship aligned with the biblical principle of being *"one flesh"* (Genesis 2:24).

In essence, understanding and valuing each other helps both spouses feel loved, secure, and deeply connected, creating an intimate bond that reflects God's original design for marriage and encourages both to thrive together in love and harmony.

Adapting Your Style to Enhance Connection

In every marriage, compromise is an essential element that helps nurture unity and understanding between spouses. This necessity for compromise is especially prominent in communication, where differing styles and preferences can sometimes lead to misunderstandings or conflict. Effective communication involves not only expressing oneself clearly but also adapting to one's partner's unique needs. This means that, while it is important to honor one's own communication style and identity, it is equally crucial to find common ground that strengthens the relationship.

Adaptation in communication does not imply losing one's individuality; rather, it encourages spouses to approach their conversations with open minds and hearts, seeking to understand and meet each other's emotional needs. For instance, if one partner thrives on clarity and directness while the other values emotional expression and nuance, it may require effort from both sides to find a balance where each feels heard and respected. This may involve the direct communicator practicing patience and active listening, while the emotionally expressive partner may need to present thoughts more clearly and succinctly.

When spouses proactively strive to meet each other's communication needs, it reflects a deep commitment to the relationship, one grounded in love and respect. Such proactivity requires awareness of each other's emotional wiring, shaped by their unique backgrounds and experiences. By engaging in this process, couples cultivate a nurturing environment where both partners can flourish, promoting intimacy and connection. The biblical principle of *"bearing with one another in love"* (Ephesians 4:2) underlines the importance of this commitment, encouraging spouses to be patient and understanding in their interactions.

Ultimately, as couples refine their communication styles and practice compromise, they build a robust foundation for a long-lasting, fulfilling marriage. By recognizing that effective communication is a mutual responsibility, both partners strengthen their emotional connection and ensure their individual needs are met. In doing so, they honor God's design for marriage, living harmoniously together and nurturing a love that mirrors the sacrificial, selfless love demonstrated in the Scriptures.

Chapter Five

The Emotional Triggers That Sabotage Conversation

Biblical Foundation: Psalm 139:23-24, Proverbs 12:16

Every marriage has moments when a simple conversation somehow turns into *that* conversation. You know the one. It starts with, *"Hey, did you move my keys?"* and ends with both of you wondering how you just revisited an argument from 2016 that neither of you remembers starting. Welcome to the world of emotional triggers, those invisible buttons that get pushed in conversation and cause reactions that seem way bigger than the words that were spoken.

Emotional triggers are rarely about the present moment alone. They're more like emotional shortcuts wired deep inside us, shaped by past experiences, unmet expectations, stress, fatigue, and sometimes hunger (never underestimate hunger). One spouse may hear a neutral comment, while the other hears criticism, rejection, or disrespect, even if none was intended. Suddenly, the conversation isn't about the dishes, the budget, or the schedule anymore; it's about feeling unappreciated, unheard, or unsafe.

The challenge in marriage is that triggers don't announce themselves politely. They don't say, *"Attention: childhood wound activated"* or *"Warning: past disappointment entering the chat."* Instead, they show up as sarcasm, defensiveness, shutdowns, raised voices, or icy silence. And often, by the time we realize we've been triggered, we've already reacted, and now we're dealing with the fallout rather than the root.

The good news is this: triggers don't have to control your conversations. When couples learn to recognize what sets them off and why, they gain the power to respond instead of react. This chapter isn't about blaming your spouse for pushing your buttons or blaming yourself for having them. It's about understanding what's really happening beneath the surface so your conversations can move from emotional minefields to opportunities for connection, growth, and most importantly, grace.

Identifying Your Personal Triggers and Reactions

Every one of us has emotional triggers, often called **"hot buttons"**, that, when pressed, send us straight to our most vulnerable place. These hot buttons are rarely random. Most of them are formed through personal pain, disappointment, rejection, trauma, or unmet needs from our past. When a hot button is pushed, we don't just hear words; we *feel* something deeper. And once emotion takes over, logic usually exits the conversation quietly and without notice.

Focus on the Family describes this dynamic as a *reactive cycle*. It's a pattern in which one spouse's emotional hot button gets pushed, triggering a reaction that then pushes the other spouse's hot button, creating a loop. The cycle doesn't require yelling or dramatic blowups, it can happen just as easily with sarcasm, defensiveness, withdrawal, or silence. The key issue is that once the cycle starts, both spouses react out of emotion rather than respond with intention.

For example, let's take Michelle and me. A conversation might start completely innocent. She may say, *"I found a pair of shoes I really like."* Then I might say, *"Did you get a chance to look at the budget today?"* On the surface, it's a neutral question. But Michelle's hot button might be *feeling criticized or overwhelmed*. That question can land as, *"You're not doing enough"* or *"You dropped the ball."* Her emotional response might be defensiveness or frustration, maybe a sharp tone or a quick explanation that sounds like justification.

Now her reaction presses *my* hot button. Mine might be *feeling disrespected or unappreciated*. I don't just hear her words; I feel attacked. So, my reactive button gets pushed, and I respond with my own defense, maybe I shut down, get sarcastic, or push back with, *"I was just asking a question."* That response then reinforces Michelle's original hot button. She feels unheard or blamed, so she reacts again. Around and around, we go.

This is where the cycle becomes self-sustaining. Each of us is no longer responding to the original topic, the budget, but to the other person's emotional reaction. Michelle's hot button (**feeling criticized**) triggers her reactive behavior (**defensiveness**), which pushes my hot button (**feeling disrespected**), triggering my reactive behavior (**withdrawal or irritation**). Each reaction feeds the next, and the conversation becomes a non-stop revolving door of emotional buttons being pressed.

And here's the sobering truth: this cycle can continue indefinitely. It doesn't stop on its own. It only stops when *one* of us recognizes what's happening and chooses to step out of the reaction. Until that happens, we can keep pushing each other's buttons for minutes, hours, or even years, often replaying the same arguments with different topics but the same emotional wounds. Understanding this cycle is the first step toward breaking it, because once you can see the pattern, you're no longer trapped by it.

Fight or Flight

When a reactive cycle is triggered between spouses, it often activates something much deeper than hurt feelings, it triggers the body's **fight-or-flight response**. This response is hard-wired into us by God for survival, designed to protect us from danger. The problem is that in marriage, the brain doesn't always know the difference between a physical threat and an emotional one. When a hot button is pushed, the body reacts as if it's under attack, and conversation quickly turns into combat or escape.

Fight responses occur when a spouse moves toward conflict to protect themselves. In conversation, this can look like raised voices, interrupting, sarcasm, lecturing, blaming, or trying to "win" the argument. The spouse in fight mode often feels a surge of adrenaline and urgency — *I have to defend myself right now.* Logic narrows, listening shuts down, and the goal quietly shifts from understanding to self-protection or control. Even when words are calm on the surface, fight can still show up as sharp tones, passive-aggressive comments, or carefully chosen phrases meant to land a blow.

Flight responses happen when a spouse moves away from the conflict to avoid emotional pain. In conversation, this often looks like withdrawal, silence, shutting down, changing the subject, leaving the room, or emotionally checking out while still physically present. The flight-oriented spouse may appear calm, but inside, they're overwhelmed. Their nervous system is saying, *"This is too much, I need out".* While flight feels safer to the person experiencing it, it often triggers the other spouse's fear of being ignored, dismissed, or abandoned, which can intensify the cycle.

Caught in these responses, spouses typically stop accurately processing the conversation. We stop listening to understand and start listening to react, or we stop listening altogether. We interrupt, rehearse our defense, bring up old issues, exaggerate language ("you always," "you never"), or retreat into silence. Empathy disappears, curiosity fades, and the original issue becomes buried under emotional self-defense. At this point, neither spouse is operating out of wisdom or love; both are operating out of fear.

The tragedy of the fight-or-flight cycle is that both responses are attempts at protection, yet both create greater distance. One spouse pushes harder, the other pulls away, and each reaction confirms the other's deepest fears. Until one spouse recognizes what's happening and intentionally slows the conversation, the reactive cycle continues, driven not by the issue at hand, but by two nervous systems desperately trying to stay safe.

Stop the cycle

To stop this dangerous and destructive cycle, the first and most critical step is **awareness.** You have to recognize the moment your hot button has been pushed. That tight feeling in your chest, the sudden urge to defend yourself, the spike in anger, or the desire to shut down are all warning lights on the dashboard. They are telling you, *this is no longer just a conversation.* Until you can name what's happening inside you, you will stay trapped in reaction mode. Scripture reminds us of this need for awareness: *"The prudent see danger and take refuge, but the simple keep going and pay the penalty"* (Proverbs 22:3).

The second step is **ownership**. This is where things get uncomfortable, but also where freedom begins. Your spouse may have pushed the button, but they are not responsible for managing your emotional well-being. You are. Blaming your spouse for your reaction keeps you powerless. Accepting responsibility puts the control back where it belongs. As Paul writes, *"Each one should test their own actions"* (Galatians 6:4). This doesn't excuse hurtful behavior, but it does acknowledge that how you respond is your choice.

Next comes the often-misunderstood step of **stepping back**. This is not withdrawing, stonewalling, or punishing your spouse with silence. It is a purposeful pause. You are choosing to pause the conversation to prevent further damage. This pause creates space to invite God into the moment through prayer, asking the Holy Spirit to calm your heart, renew your mind, and reveal what's really stirring inside you. *"Be still and know that I am God"* (Psalm 46:10) is not just a spiritual idea — it's a relational lifeline.

Once you've paused, it's time to **attend to your feelings**. Ask yourself honest questions: *What am I actually feeling right now? Why did this hit me so hard? What past pain or fear is being activated?* The goal isn't to justify your reaction, but to understand it. David modeled this kind of emotional honesty before God when he prayed, *"Search me, God, and know my heart; test me and know my anxious thoughts"* (Psalm 139:23). When you can name the emotion — hurt, fear, rejection, insecurity — you begin to regain clarity and self-control.

Only after this inner work has begun are you ready to **re-engage**. And when you do, the goal is no longer to win, defend, or be proven right, but to pursue peace and restoration. You come back calmer, clearer, and more humble, able to speak truth in love (Ephesians 4:15). You listen to understand, not to react. You take responsibility for your part and extend grace for theirs. *"A gentle answer turns away wrath, but a harsh word stirs up anger"* (Proverbs 15:1).

This is how the reactive cycle is broken, not by overpowering your spouse, but by surrendering your reactions to God. When you slow down, take responsibility, invite the Holy Spirit into the process, and then re-engage with wisdom and love, you transform conflict from a destructive force into an opportunity for healing, growth, and deeper connection.

For a more in-depth look at the reactive cycle and the care cycle to break it, visit www.reactivecycle.com. There, you can take an assessment to identify your triggers and put into motion a care cycle to improve your communication with your spouse.

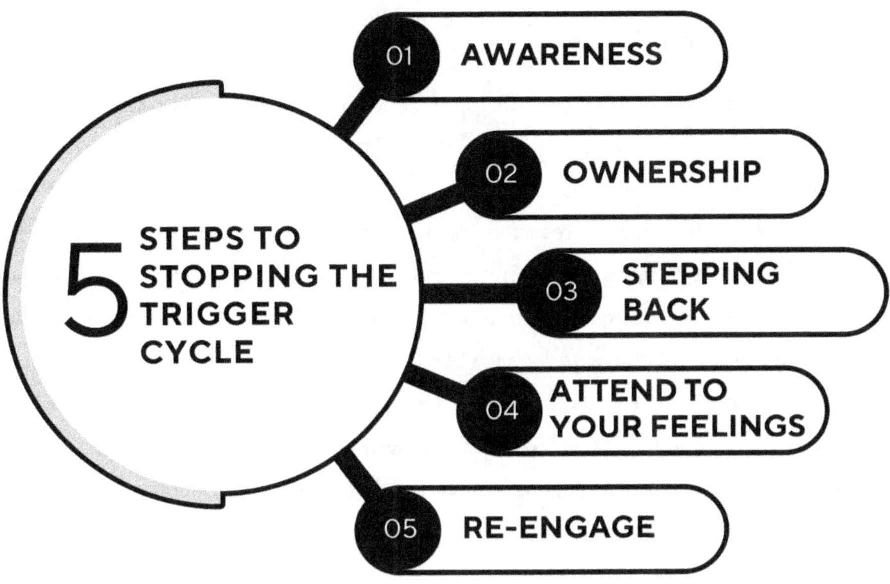

Understanding the Roots of Defensiveness

Defensiveness is one of the most common reactions we experience when an emotional trigger is activated, and research shows it is rooted in our brain's instinct to protect our self-worth and emotional safety. When we perceive criticism, whether real or imagined, the nervous system can interpret it as a threat, especially if past pain, rejection, or unresolved trauma are involved. In that moment, the goal quietly shifts from understanding our spouse to protecting ourselves. This is why defensiveness often shows up as **justifying**, **explaining**, **blaming**, **minimizing**, or **counterattacking**. For example, Michelle and I might be talking about something simple, like household responsibilities. If Michelle says, *"I feel like I'm carrying most of the load lately,"* my hot button of feeling unappreciated can get pushed. Instead of hearing her emotion, I may react defensively with, *"That's not fair, I do plenty around here,"* trying to protect my image rather than understand her heart. That defensive reaction then communicates dismissal, which can trigger her fear of being unheard or unsupported, further escalating the cycle.

Defensiveness is damaging in marriage because it shuts down real listening and invalidates your spouse's experience. Rather than creating safety, it creates distance. Conversations turn into debates rather than dialogues, and the focus shifts from what is true to who is right. Scripture warns us about this dynamic, reminding us to be *"quick to listen, slow to speak, and slow to become angry"* (James 1:19). To avoid defensiveness, the conversation must be intentionally restructured in the moment. This means slowing down, acknowledging that a trigger has been hit, and choosing curiosity over self-protection. Instead of defending myself, I might respond to Michelle with, "It sounds like you're overwhelmed, help me understand what's been weighing on you." This kind of response invites connection rather than conflict and reflects a godly posture of humility, grace, and love. When we surrender our need to defend ourselves and invite the Holy Spirit to guide our words, we create space for healing, understanding, and unity rather than continuing a cycle that only deepens the divide.

How Unmet Expectations Fuel Conflict

One of the most dangerous, and often most naïve issues in marriage when it comes to conversation is **unmet expectations**. Expectations themselves are not the problem; the real danger lies in *unspoken* expectations. Many couples quietly carry assumptions about what their spouse *should* know, *should* do, or *should* understand without ever clearly expressing those expectations. When those assumptions aren't met, disappointment sets in, and that disappointment often turns into frustration, resentment, or emotional withdrawal.

The disconnect usually begins when spouses expect each other to be mind readers. One spouse thinks that *if they really loved me, they would know*, while the other is completely unaware that an expectation even exists. Over time, these silent expectations create an invisible scoreboard, one spouse feels let down, while the other feels confused or blindsided by the tension. Instead of addressing the real issue, conversations become loaded with emotion, vague complaints, or passive comments that mask the true unmet need.

Unmet expectations are especially destructive because they often masquerade as character flaws. A spouse may interpret unmet expectations as a lack of care, effort, or love, when in reality the issue is a lack of clarity. Scripture reminds us of the importance of clear communication:

"Plans fail for lack of counsel, but with many advisers they succeed" (Proverbs 20:18). In marriage, your spouse is not an adviser who can guess your plans, they need to hear them.

Unmet and unknown expectations are powerful fuel for conflict because they create emotional reactions without ever revealing the real cause. When expectations are unspoken, a spouse has no opportunity to meet them, yet they are often judged as if they intentionally failed. Over time, this produces frustration and hurt on one side and confusion or defensiveness on the other. The conflict that follows is rarely about the surface issue being discussed; it is about the disappointment and unmet needs simmering underneath. What makes this especially destructive is that neither spouse may fully understand why the tension keeps showing up, they only feel its effects.

As these unmet expectations accumulate, they begin to distort how spouses interpret each other's actions. Neutral behaviors are filtered through disappointment and can be misread as indifference, selfishness, or lack of love. A spouse may start assuming negative intent: *"They don't care,"* *"I'm not a priority,"* or *"I'm always alone in this."* These assumptions harden into beliefs, which in turn shape the tone and posture of future conversations. Instead of curiosity and grace, spouses bring suspicion and emotional armor into every interaction.

Left unchecked, this pattern breeds resentment, which is one of the most corrosive forces in marriage. Resentment quietly erodes goodwill, patience, and empathy. Small issues trigger big reactions because they tap into a reservoir of unmet expectations that have never been addressed. Conversations become tense, defensive, or avoidant, and emotional intimacy begins to fade. As Scripture warns, *"Catch for us the foxes, the little foxes that ruin the vineyards"* (Song of Songs 2:15). Unspoken expectations are often those "little foxes", small, hidden, but devastating over time.

Ultimately, unmet and unacknowledged expectations can destroy a marriage by replacing honest communication with silent disappointment. Instead of working as a team, spouses drift into isolation, each carrying their own unvoiced needs and assumptions.

Without intentional effort to bring expectations into the open, couples can end up living parallel lives, sharing a home but not a heart. Healing begins when expectations are spoken, clarified, and surrendered to God, allowing grace, understanding, and unity to take the place of assumption and resentment.

Healthy, godly communication replaces assumptions with honesty. Instead of expecting mind-reading, spouses must learn to express their needs, desires, and expectations with humility and grace. When expectations are spoken clearly, they can be discussed, adjusted, or agreed upon. When they remain unspoken, they quietly erode connection and trust. Bringing expectations into the light transforms them from hidden landmines into opportunities for understanding, alignment, and deeper unity.

Recognizing When Past Pain Hijacks Present Communication

Another significant source of communication breakdown in marriage occurs when past pain and emotional trauma hijack present conversations. In these moments, a spouse is no longer responding only to what is being said in the here and now but is reacting to something from their past. Old wounds quietly take over the interaction, often without either person realizing it. What looks like an overreaction in the moment is often a protective response shaped by earlier experiences.

Emotional trauma, whether from childhood, previous relationships, betrayal, neglect, or repeated unresolved conflict, creates internal triggers. When a current conversation brushes against one of those triggers, the brain can shift into a defensive or protective mode. Instead of listening with openness, the person subconsciously prepares to avoid being hurt again. The conversation stops being about understanding and starts being about self-protection.

From a neurological perspective, this often happens when the amygdala, the brain's threat detector, overrides the prefrontal cortex, which is responsible for reasoning, empathy, and thoughtful communication. When this occurs, communication becomes reactive rather than reflective. Words come faster than wisdom, and emotions lead instead of understanding.

A practical example of this might be a husband saying to his wife, *"Hey, can we talk about the budget this month? I'm a little concerned."* On the surface, this is a neutral and reasonable request. However, if the wife grew up in a home where money conversations always led to criticism, control, or shame, her brain may interpret his words as an attack rather than an invitation to talk. Internally, she may hear, *"You're irresponsible," "You're failing,"* or *"You're about to be criticized."*

As a result, her response may seem out of proportion to the situation. She might become defensive and say, *"Why do you always make this my fault?"* She may shut down completely, responding with silence, withdrawal, or avoidance. Or she may escalate emotionally with anger, sarcasm, or tears. To the husband, the reaction feels confusing and excessive. To her nervous system, however, she is protecting herself from an old pain that feels very real in that moment.

When past pain hijacks communication regularly, couples often notice consistent patterns. These may include overreactions to relatively small comments, conversations that escalate or shut down quickly, feeling deeply misunderstood even when intentions are good, and repeated arguments that follow the same emotional script. Phrases like "You always" or "You never" often surface, signaling that the conversation has shifted from the present issue to unresolved emotional history.

Scripture speaks clearly to the reality that what happens in the heart shapes what comes out in communication. Proverbs 4:23 reminds us *"to guard our hearts, because everything we do flows from them."* When the heart carries unhealed wounds, those wounds influence tone, words, and reactions. Ephesians 4:26 warns against letting anger linger, pointing to the danger of unresolved emotions that can resurface later in destructive ways. James 1:19 calls believers *"to be quick to listen, slow to speak, and slow to become angry"*, an instruction that requires emotional awareness and restraint, especially when old pain is activated.

Modern research and counseling studies reinforce these biblical principles. They show that emotional awareness is one of the most effective tools for preventing past pain from controlling present conversations. When a person learns to recognize and name their triggers, acknowledging that a reaction may be connected to something older, it reduces the power of that trigger. Awareness interrupts the automatic emotional cycle.

Studies also show that slowing conversations down is critical. Pausing, taking deep breaths, stepping away briefly, or praying silently helps calm the nervous system and reengage rational thinking. Couples who create space instead of pushing through heightened emotions communicate more effectively and with less damage.

Another proven strategy is learning to engage in safe, non-defensive dialogue. Research consistently shows that "I feel" statements are far more effective than accusations. Saying, *"I feel anxious when money comes up,"* invites understanding, while blame invites defensiveness. Healthy communication focuses on sharing internal experiences rather than assigning fault.

Addressing the root of emotional pain is also essential. **Counseling, pastoral care, journaling,** and **prayer that focus on healing past wounds** significantly reduce emotional hijacking in future conversations. When the wound heals, the trigger loses its intensity. Couples are no longer fighting old battles in new conversations.

Finally, research highlights the importance of grace and curiosity in relationships. Healthy couples learn to ask, *"What might this reaction be connected to?"* rather than *"Why are you acting like this?"* This posture encourages empathy, patience, and connection rather than judgment.

When past pain hijacks present communication, couples are rarely just disagreeing over the topic at hand. They are encountering an unhealed place in the heart. The gospel offers both truth and grace, truth to recognize what is happening beneath the surface, and grace to respond with compassion, patience, and love. As healing takes place through prayer, honest dialogue, and intentional growth, communication becomes less reactive and more reflective of the unity and peace God designed for marriage.

Inviting the Holy Spirit to Heal Emotional Patterns

At the deepest level, lasting healing in our communication failures does not begin with better techniques or stronger arguments but with inviting the Holy Spirit to work in our hearts and conversations. Scripture teaches that transformation starts internally: *"Create in me a clean heart, O God, and renew a right spirit within me"* (Psalm 51:10). When we invite the Holy Spirit to examine and heal our emotional patterns, our fears, wounds, pride, and defensiveness, He begins to reshape the source from which our words flow. Jesus reminds us that *"out of the abundance of the heart the mouth speaks"* (Luke 6:45), meaning unresolved heart issues will inevitably surface in our communication. The Holy Spirit convicts, comforts, and renews, replacing reactive patterns with the fruit of the Spirit, love, patience, gentleness, self-control, and peace (Galatians 5:22–23). As we yield our emotions and responses to Him, He teaches us how to listen with humility, speak with grace, and respond rather than react. Jesus promised, *"Peace I leave with you; my peace I give to you"* (John 14:27), a peace not dependent on winning arguments but on surrendered hearts. When the Spirit is invited into our lives and conversations, He heals the emotional baggage that silently shapes our reactions, aligns our responses with Christ's character, and leads us into true peace and resolution, peace that cannot be manufactured by human effort but only received through daily dependence on Him.

As we close this chapter, it becomes clear that communication breakdowns are rarely just about words, they are about hearts. When emotional wounds, unresolved patterns, and unmet expectations go unaddressed, they quietly shape the way we listen, speak, and respond. True healing and lasting change begin when we invite the Holy Spirit to do the deep work that only He can, restoring our hearts and renewing how we engage one another. As we learn to surrender our communication to God, we create space for grace, understanding, and peace to replace fear, defensiveness, and division.

In the next chapter, we will take this foundation a step further by exploring how conflict itself can become a powerful tool for growth rather than a source of harm. We will talk about how to engage in conflict that connects, learning how to fight in a God-honoring way that strengthens intimacy, deepens trust, and reflects Christ's love even in moments of disagreement.

Chapter Six

Good Conflict: Disagreeing in a God-Honoring Way

Biblical Foundation: Ephesians 4:26-27, Matthew 18:15, Romans 12:18

Healthy, **God-honoring conflict in marriage** isn't about avoiding disagreement — it's about how we *engage* in it. When handled with love, respect, and humility, conflict becomes an opportunity for deeper intimacy, mutual growth, and greater unity rather than division.

At its core, conflict reveals the places where two imperfect people are trying to reconcile their different needs, desires, or perspectives. When couples approach these moments with a **spirit of cooperation rather than competition**, they model Christlike humility and a servant's heart. Instead of keeping score or trying to "win," they listen, seek understanding, validate feelings, and work toward solutions that honor both partners. This is consistent with biblical teachings: Ephesians 4:2-3 calls believers to be *"completely humble and gentle; be patient, bearing with one another in love"* as they maintain unity. When couples intentionally apply these principles, conflict can strengthen trust, deepen emotional safety, and clarify each other's values and limits.

From a psychological perspective, not all conflict is created equal. Research distinguishes between **constructive conflict, where couple's express concerns directly and respectfully, and destructive conflict, marked by criticism, withdrawal, or**

hostility. Constructive conflict has been linked to **improved problem-solving and higher relationship satisfaction**, especially when serious issues are addressed openly, and partners are willing to change. By contrast, chronic tension and unresolved negativity are associated with poorer marital quality and a higher risk of dissolution over time. What this tells us is that conflict itself isn't inherently bad — what matters is *how* it's handled.

A few ways healthy conflict can *actually be good* for a marriage include:

- **Improved communication skills:** Working through disagreements teaches couples to articulate needs, listen actively, and express vulnerability without fear.

- **Increased emotional intimacy:** When spouses feel heard and respected, trust deepens, and both feel safer to share honestly.

- **Clarified expectations and boundaries:** Conflict can spotlight unspoken assumptions, helping couples negotiate roles, responsibilities, and priorities more clearly.

- **Stronger conflict resolution habits:** Repeatedly resolving differences constructively builds confidence in the relationship's resilience.

Some research also shows that conflict-resolution skills are tied to long-term well-being. For example, studies show that couples who use positive conflict strategies tend to experience greater satisfaction and healthier interactions over time. In contrast, negative conflict patterns are linked to stress and reduced marital quality.

While it's hard to capture the "right" number of conflicts a marriage should have, broader social data show that divorce, which is often the outcome of unresolved, chronic tension, remains significant: in the United States, over **1.8 million Americans divorced in 2023**, and about **one-third of adults who have ever been married have experienced a divorce** at some point in their lives. This reveals that addressing conflict well isn't just a nice idea, it's essential to relational longevity.

In a Christian marriage, conflict also invites spiritual growth. It pushes both partners toward forgiveness, patience, and Christ-centered reconciliation. When couples pray together about disagreements, seek wisdom from Scripture rather than their own instincts, and choose to forgive quickly, they practice the same grace God extends to them. Over time, what once was a point of contention can become a testimony of redemption and unity, illustrating that conflict handled well doesn't *weaken* a marriage, it *refines* it.

Shifting From "Winning" to "Understanding"

In a healthy, God-centered marriage, spouses are not opponents locked in a debate, they are **best friends on the same team**. Scripture paints marriage as a covenant of unity, not competition: *"The two shall become one"* (Genesis 2:24). When we remember that truth, it reshapes how we communicate, especially in conflict. If Michelle and I are truly one, then attacking her perspective is, in a sense, attacking myself. God-honoring communication protects the friendship at the heart of marriage by choosing words, tone, and posture that build rather than bruise, even when emotions are high and agreement feels far away.

This is where mindset matters. Many conflicts escalate not because the issue is unsolvable, but because one or both spouses enter the conversation focused on **winning instead of understanding**. Winning says, *"I need to prove I'm right."* Understanding says, *"I need to understand your heart."* James 1:19 gives clear guidance here: *"Everyone should be quick to listen, slow to speak and slow to become angry."* When couples shift from winning to understanding, the goal moves from domination to connection. The question is no longer, *"How do I convince you?"* but *"Help me see what you're seeing."*

Some spouses, by personality and wiring, are strong-willed, decisive, and driven. These traits can be tremendous strengths in leadership, work, and problem-solving. But in marriage, that same drive can quietly turn conversations into contests. A win-at-all-costs mentality may secure a short-term victory in an argument, but it often creates long-term damage in trust, safety, and emotional closeness. Even if one spouse "wins" the point, the relationship loses when the other feels unheard, dismissed, or overpowered. In marriage, **being right is far less important than being righteous in how we treat each other.**

Here's what this can look like in practice. Imagine Michelle and I are in conflict over a decision, maybe scheduling, finances, or how to handle a family responsibility. My natural tendency might be to push hard for my solution, explaining why it's logical, efficient, and "makes the most sense." Michelle, on the other hand, may be expressing emotional concerns, stress, or priorities that feel just as real to her. If I approach the conversation with the goal of winning, I might interrupt, defend, or dismiss her feelings as secondary to the solution. At that point, even if she eventually agrees, she hasn't truly been valued, and our friendship takes a hit.

But if I pause and shift my mindset, the conversation changes. Instead of arguing my point, I might say, *"Michelle, help me understand what's weighing on you about this. I want to know what you're feeling, not just what you're thinking."* That simple posture invites safety. Michelle can then share freely, knowing she's not in a courtroom defending her case. I may still hold a different opinion at the end, and she may still disagree with me, but now we understand each other. We can look for a solution that honors both perspectives, or at least agree on the next step with mutual respect.

In that moment, **both of us win**, even without full agreement. Michelle wins because she is heard and valued. I win because I protect our friendship and unity. And our marriage wins because conflict didn't turn us into enemies, it reminded us we are partners. God-honoring communication doesn't require perfect agreement; it requires a shared commitment to love, humility, and understanding. When couples fight *for* each other instead of *against* each other, conflict becomes a tool that strengthens the bond rather than strains it.

Here are quick, practical options couples can use to approach difficult conversations in a way that keeps the focus on *working through the issue* rather than *taking control of it*. Each one helps shift the heart posture from urgency and dominance to understanding and unity and each produces a better long-term outcome in marriage.

1. Pause Before You Press

Instead of reacting immediately, choose to pause, even briefly, before responding. This creates space for the Holy Spirit to check motives and calm emotions.

"Be still and know that I am God." (Psalm 46:10)
"Everyone should be quick to listen, slow to speak, and slow to become angry." (James 1:19)

Pausing prevents conversations from becoming emotional collisions. It communicates, *"You matter more than my need to respond right now."* This tone encourages safety rather than defensiveness and helps prevent conflict from spiraling out of control.

2. Lead With Curiosity, Not Certainty

Approach the conversation with questions instead of conclusions:

- "Help me understand what you're feeling."

- "What's most important to you in this?"

- "What am I missing here?"

"The purposes of a person's heart are deep waters, but one who has insight draws them out." (Proverbs 20:5)

Curiosity lowers walls. It tells your spouse they are not an obstacle to overcome but a heart to be understood. Understanding doesn't require agreement — it requires humility.

3. Name the Team You're On

Verbally remind each other that you're not enemies:

- "We're on the same team."

- "I don't want to win — I want us to be okay."

- "Let's protect our marriage while we talk about this."

"A cord of three strands is not quickly broken." (Ecclesiastes 4:12)

When couples name unity out loud, it reframes the conversation. Conflict stops being a battle and becomes a joint problem-solving effort, strengthening trust instead of eroding it.

4. Slow the Pace on Purpose

Strong personalities often rush in like a bull in a China closet, not because they don't care, but because they want resolution fast. Intentionally slowing the conversation protects the relationship.

"Plans fail for lack of counsel, but with many advisers they succeed." (Proverbs 20:18)

Slowing down prevents emotional damage. It allows both spouses to process, reflect, and respond thoughtfully instead of reactively. Clarity almost always improves with time.

5. Validate Before You Evaluate

Before offering solutions or defending your position, acknowledge your spouse's experience:

- "That makes sense."

- "I can see why you'd feel that way."

- "Thank you for telling me that."

"Carry each other's burdens, and in this way, you will fulfill the law of Christ." (Galatians 6:2)

Validation doesn't mean agreement — it means respect. When someone feels heard, they're far more open to collaboration and compromise.

6. Invite God into the Middle of the Moment

Even a short prayer can reset the atmosphere:

- "Lord, help us love each other well right now."

- "Give us wisdom and patience."

"If any of you lacks wisdom, you should ask God." (James 1:5)

Prayer shifts focus from control to surrender. It reminds both spouses that the goal isn't domination — it's Christlike love and unity.

The Bigger Picture: Setting the Tone for the Future

When couples consistently choose understanding over urgency, conflict stops being something to dread. Each resolved disagreement becomes **proof that the marriage is safe**, that both hearts matter, and that growth is possible. Over time, this approach trains the relationship to associate conflict with **connection instead of fear**.

"Let us therefore make every effort to do what leads to peace and to mutual edification." (Romans 14:19)

Handled this way, conflict becomes a **trust-building rhythm** — not a threat. Each conversation lays the groundwork for the next, teaching both spouses: *We can face hard things together.* And that confidence, rooted in God-honoring communication, is what allows a marriage not just to survive conflict, but to grow stronger through it.

How to Bring Up Issues Without Blame

In the book *The Mindful Marriage*, Ron and Nancy Deal explain that every person brings a built-in response mechanism into marriage, especially in moments of stress and conflict. These responses often show up as **blame, shame, control, or escape**. While they may feel instinctive or even protective in the moment, none of them lead to healthy, God-honoring conflict. Instead of moving a couple toward understanding and unity, they tend to harden hearts, escalate tension, and damage trust.

Blame is one of the most common and de-structive responses in marriage conflicts. When an issue is raised primarily to point a finger, *"This is your fault"* or *"If you would just change..."*, the conversation immediately becomes adversarial. Blame shifts the focus away from solving the problem and onto defending oneself. Scripture warns against this posture in Proverbs 18:17, which reminds us that *"In a lawsuit the first to speak seems right, until someone comes forward and cross-examines."* When blame dominates, listening disappears, humility evaporates, and the marriage becomes a courtroom rather than a partnership.

Shame, whether directed inward or outward, is equally harmful. When a spouse feels shamed, made to feel defective, inadequate, or "not enough", they are far less likely to engage openly or honestly. Shame attacks identity rather than addressing behavior, which contradicts God's heart for restoration and grace. Romans 8:1 reminds us that *"there is now no condemnation for those who are in Christ Jesus."* A marriage marked by shame creates fear and withdrawal, not safety and growth.

Control often emerges when one spouse believes the best way to fix conflict is to force an outcome, pushing harder, talking louder, or insisting on their solution. While control can create short-term compliance, it erodes long-term connection. Control communicates, *"My way matters more than your heart,"* which undermines the oneness marriage is meant to reflect. Philippians 2:3 calls couples to *"do nothing out of selfish ambition or vain conceit, but in humility consider others better than yourselves."* Control may feel efficient, but it comes at the cost of intimacy.

Escape is the opposite extreme, withdrawing emotionally, shutting down, avoiding the conversation altogether, or physically leaving the conflict unresolved. While escape can reduce immediate tension, it can also allow problems to fester and grow. Avoidance doesn't bring peace; it simply delays pain. Ephesians 4:26 cautions believers not to let the sun go down on unresolved anger, emphasizing the importance of addressing issues rather than burying them.

When couples consistently raise issues in ways that assign blame or rely on reactive patterns, conflict stops being productive and becomes corrosive. God-honoring conflict requires a different approach, one rooted in humility, responsibility, and grace. Instead of asking, *"How do I prove my spouse is wrong?"* the healthier question becomes, *"What is my role in this, and how can we work through it together?"* By recognizing and resisting these default responses, couples create space for understanding, healing, and growth, turning conflict from a threat into an opportunity to strengthen the marriage God has entrusted to them.

Let's take a look at what blame can look like, and then we'll look at some bullet points on how to solve it. I will use Michelle and me as an example.

What Blame Sounds Like in a Conflict

Blame language usually focuses on *what the other person did wrong* and implies intent or character flaws.

Example (Blame-Filled Conversation):

- **Me:** "You never listen to me. Every time I talk, you're on your phone."

- **Michelle:** "That's not true. You always pick the worst times to talk, and then you get mad at me."

- **Me:** "See? You're doing it right now. You don't care how I feel."

- **Michelle:** "And you're just trying to control what I do."

Notice the pattern:

- "You never..."

- "You always..."

- Mind-reading ("you don't care")

- Character attacks ("controlling")

This language **creates defense, not understanding**.

The First Correction: Removing Blame with I-Statements

A common corrective step is to use I-statements, which shift the focus from accusations to personal experience.

Blame → I-Statement

- Instead of: "You never listen to me."

- Say this: "I feel unheard when I'm talking and there are distractions."

That's a *huge* improvement, but there's an important caveat.

The "Secondary You" Problem (Important for Couples)

Even I-statements can **smuggle in blame if they include what many counselors call a secondary 'you'.**

Examples of I-Statements with Hidden Blame:

- "I feel frustrated **when you ignore me.**"

- "I feel disrespected **because you don't prioritize me.**"

- "I feel hurt **by what you did.**"

These still point the finger, just more politely.

Cleaner, Blame-Free I-Statements:

- "I feel frustrated **when I don't feel engaged with.**"

- "I feel disconnected **when a lot is going on around us.**"

- "I feel hurt **when I interpret the moment as unimportant.**"

The shift:

- From **what you did**

- To **what I experienced**

Other Proven Ways to Communicate Without Blame

Beyond I-statements, studies on marital communication highlight several **effective, blame-free tools**:

Describe, Don't Diagnose

- Instead of: "You're selfish."

- Say this: "When the decision was made without talking, I felt left out."

Stick to **observable behavior**, not motives or character.

Use Soft Start-Ups

Conversations that begin gently are far more likely to end well.

- Instead of: "Why do you always do this?"

- Say this: "Can we talk about something that's been on my mind?"

Tone matters as much as words.

Validate Before Responding

Validation doesn't mean agreement, it means understanding.

- "I can see why that felt overwhelming to you."

- "That makes sense given how your day went."

Feeling understood lowers defensiveness almost immediately.

Speak in Needs, Not Complaints

- Instead of: "You don't make time for me."

- Say this: "I need intentional time together to feel connected."

Needs invite partnership. Complaints invite resistance.

Take Responsibility for Your Part

Even partial ownership reduces blame.

- "I realize I came in frustrated, and that probably set the tone."

- "I didn't communicate my expectations clearly."

Humility changes the emotional climate.

Why Removing Blame Creates a Safe Space (The Big Picture)

Blame triggers **self-protection**.
Safety invites **connection**.

When blame is present:

- Hearts close

- Walls go up

- The real issue never gets addressed

When blame is removed:

- Both spouses stay emotionally open

- Listening replaces defending

- Solutions become possible

A blame-free conversation says:
"You are safe with me, even when we disagree."

That safety allows couples to:

- Address the real problem

- Learn from each other

- Walk away with clarity instead of resentment

Blame doesn't bring change — it brings walls. But when we remove blame, we create a safe space where hearts stay open, truth can be heard, and real progress can finally happen.

On a side note, I highly recommend you purchase Ron and Nancy Deal's book, *"The Mindful Marriage."* It is one of the best books I have found that resonates not only with first marriages but also with blended families. It is well worth the purchase.

Using Biblical Peacemaking Principles in Marriage

No matter how many communication tools, techniques, or conflict-resolution strategies we learn, one of the safest and most effective places we can always run to for learning how to communicate and live in unity within our marriages is the Bible, God's Word. Scripture doesn't simply give us rules for conversation; it reshapes our hearts so that our words reflect Christ. Jesus reminds us that *"out of the abundance of the heart the mouth speaks"* (Matthew 12:34). This means our communication struggles are often heart issues first, not just language issues, and lasting change begins when we allow God to work internally before we speak externally.

God's Word consistently calls us to humility, which is essential for peace in marriage. Pride fuels conflict, but humility disarms it. Philippians 2:3 instructs us to *"value others above ourselves"*, and when we apply that truth in marriage, the goal shifts from winning an argument to protecting the relationship. Humility allows us to listen with an open heart rather than react defensively. Jesus modeled this perfectly, describing Himself as gentle and humble in heart (Matthew 11:29). When humility guides our conversations, tension decreases and understanding increases.

Scripture also emphasizes the importance of guarding our words. The Bible reminds us that the *"tongue carries the power of life and death"* (Proverbs 18:21), which means our words can either heal or harm our marriage. Ephesians 4:29 calls us to *"speak in ways that build up rather than tear down"*, especially during moments of disagreement. James 1:19 further encourages us to be *"quick to listen, slow to speak, and slow to become angry."* When we allow these truths to shape our conversations, we create an environment where peace can grow rather than conflict escalate.

God does not call married couples to avoid conflict, but to pursue peace intentionally. Jesus teaches that *"peacemakers are blessed and recognized as children of God"* (Matthew 5:9). Romans 12:18 reminds us that, as much as it depends on us, *"we are to live at peace with others"*. In marriage, this means choosing unity over pride and reconciliation over being right. Peacekeeping in a biblical sense is not passive; it is an active pursuit of love, patience, and understanding, even when emotions are high.

Forgiveness is another cornerstone of biblical communication and peacekeeping in marriage. Unforgiveness hardens hearts and poisons conversations, but God calls us to *"forgive just as we have been forgiven through Christ"* (Ephesians 4:32). First Peter 4:8 reminds us that *"love covers a multitude of sins, not by ignoring issues, but by responding with grace."* When forgiveness becomes a regular practice in marriage, past wounds no longer drive conversations, and spouses feel safe to be honest without fear of condemnation.

Love must remain the motivation behind every conversation. First Corinthians 13 describes love as patient, kind, and not easily angered, and says that love keeps no record of wrongs. When love governs our communication, we slow down, soften our tone, and refuse to weaponize mistakes from the past. Husbands are specifically called to *"love their wives as Christ loved the church, with sacrificial and selfless devotion"* (Ephesians 5:25). That same Christlike love is meant to define every interaction between spouses.

Finally, Scripture reminds us that true peace does not come from perfect communication but from inviting God into our conversations. Philippians 4:6-7 encourages us to *"bring everything to God in prayer, promising that His peace will guard our hearts and minds."* When couples pray together, especially before or during difficult conversations, they create space for God's peace to settle emotions and protect hearts from closing off. A marriage grounded in prayer is one where communication becomes safer, calmer, and more productive.

When God's Word shapes our hearts, it naturally shapes our communication. Humility replaces pride, grace replaces blame, forgiveness replaces resentment, and peace replaces tension. Applying biblical principles to marriage communication creates a safe space where hearts remain open, truth can be shared in love, and unity can flourish. When couples allow Scripture to lead their conversations, they don't just talk better, they grow closer, stronger, and more aligned with God's design for marriage.

Resolving Tension Before it Turns into Resentment

When tension between spouses goes unresolved or is handled in unhealthy ways, it rarely just disappears. Instead, it often settles quietly into the heart and slowly turns into resentment. Resentment is not usually born from one major conflict but from many small moments of tension that were ignored, dismissed, or mishandled. Scripture warns us about this progression when it says, *"Be angry and do not sin; do not let the sun go down on your anger"* (Ephesians 4:26). God knows that unresolved anger doesn't stay neutral — it grows.

For example, imagine Michelle sharing something with me that's important to her, but I'm distracted and respond half-heartedly. She feels brushed off but doesn't say anything in the moment because she doesn't want to start an argument. Later that same week, something small happens, maybe I forget to follow through, and her reaction feels stronger than the situation warrants. What's really happening isn't about that moment; it's about the earlier tension that was never addressed. That unspoken hurt quietly turned into frustration and, if left unchecked, would eventually harden into resentment.

Healthy resolution begins by addressing tension early, gently, and honestly. Instead of holding it in, Michelle could say, *"When I was sharing earlier and felt like I didn't have your full attention, it made me feel unimportant. Can we talk about that?"* That kind of response doesn't accuse; it invites connection. Proverbs 15:1 reminds us that *"a gentle answer turns away wrath,"* and that gentleness creates space for understanding rather than defensiveness.

When tension is addressed promptly, it allows both spouses to stay emotionally connected. I might respond by acknowledging my part and saying, *"I'm sorry. I didn't realize how that came across, but I can see how that hurt you."* Even owning a small piece of responsibility helps relieve emotional pressure before it has a chance to build. James 5:16 encourages confession and openness because healing happens when things are brought into the light.

Resolving tension early also protects the heart. Hebrews 12:15 warns us to watch out for a root of bitterness that can grow and cause trouble. Resentment is that root, it grows quietly but affects everything. When Michelle and I choose to pause, address the tension, and seek understanding rather than avoidance, we stop resentment before it takes hold.

In marriage, peace is preserved not by never having tension, but by handling it well when it arises. When we choose honest, humble, and timely communication, we keep small issues from becoming big wounds. Addressing tension early keeps hearts soft, trust strong, and love growing, rather than allowing resentment to reshape the relationship quietly.

> **Tension in marriage isn't a sign you're breaking apart—it's often the pressure God uses to press you closer together**

Restoring Unity After an Argument

This chapter may feel heavy because it has asked us to slow down, look inward, and honestly examine how we communicate, handle tension, and respond to conflict in a God-honoring way. Those kinds of conversations are rarely easy, but they are necessary. The hope is that by becoming more aware of these patterns and intentionally putting some of these processes into action, real fruit will begin to grow in your marriage. Awareness is often the first step toward change. When you recognize unhealthy dynamics as they arise rather than after damage is done, you can respond with wisdom, grace, and purpose rather than emotion alone.

As we close this chapter, it's important to acknowledge that even when couples handle conflict better, arguments can still leave behind feelings of disconnection, frustration, or lingering anger. That emotional distance after a disagreement is common, but it doesn't have to be permanent. Scripture reminds us not to let unresolved anger linger because it opens the door to bitterness and division (Ephesians 4:26–27). God's desire is not just that we stop arguing, but that we actively work toward restoration and unity after the argument has passed.

RESTORING UNITY AFTER AN ARGUMENT

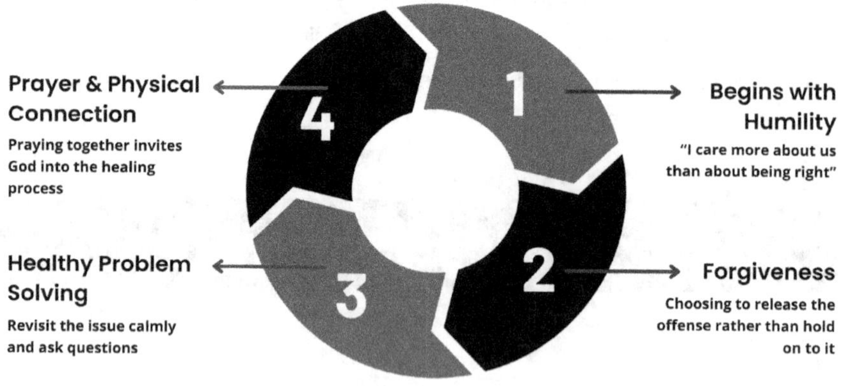

Restoring unity begins with humility. Someone must be willing to take the first step, even if both spouses feel hurt. Humility says, *"I care more about us than about being right."* Philippians 2:3 calls us to value one another above ourselves, and that often means revisiting a hard moment with a softer heart. This might look like acknowledging your part in the conflict, apologizing sincerely, or simply saying, *"I don't want there to be distance between us."*

Biblical restoration also requires forgiveness. Forgiveness is not minimizing the issue or pretending the hurt didn't happen; it is choosing to release the offense rather than hold onto it. Colossians 3:13 reminds us to *"forgive as the Lord forgave us."* When forgiveness is offered and received, it clears the emotional debris left behind by conflict and makes room for reconnection.

After forgiveness, healthy problem-solving can take place. Once emotions have settled, couples can revisit the issue calmly and ask questions like, *"What can we do differently next time?"* or *"What do we both need moving forward?"* Proverbs 20:5 reminds us that understanding takes effort, but it is worth drawing out. These conversations are not about reopening wounds, but about learning and growing together.

Finally, unity is often restored most powerfully through prayer and physical reconnection. Praying together after an argument invites God into the healing process and reminds both spouses that they are on the same team, under the same Lord. God's peace, promised in Philippians 4:7, guards hearts that are surrendered to Him. Simple gestures, like a hug, holding hands, or sitting together, can also help rebuild emotional closeness and signal that the relationship is safe again.

In closing this chapter, remember that conflict does not have to be the enemy of your marriage. When handled biblically and intentionally, it can become a doorway to deeper understanding, stronger trust, and greater unity. By addressing issues as they arise, resolving tension with humility and grace, and intentionally restoring connection after disagreements, couples can experience growth instead of division. Heavy conversations can produce beautiful results when God's wisdom leads the way.

Chapter Seven

Difficult Conversations Made Easier

Biblical Foundation: Proverbs 27:6, Galatians 6:1

No one enters marriage *wanting* difficult conversations. Most couples hope love will smooth over disagreements and that shared faith, good intentions, and time together will keep conflict to a minimum. Yet the reality of marriage is that two unique people, with different backgrounds, expectations, personalities, and communication styles, are learning to become one. That process makes difficult conversations not just likely, but unavoidable.

Marriage touches every part of life: finances, intimacy, parenting, boundaries, faith, priorities, and personal growth. As seasons change, new pressures arise, and unspoken expectations surface, moments of tension naturally follow. Avoiding hard conversations may feel like peace in the short term, but over time, it often creates distance, misunderstanding, and unresolved hurt. Scripture reminds us that growth and maturity rarely come without effort. Proverbs 27:17 says, *"As iron sharpens iron, so one person sharpens another."* Sharpening, by nature, involves friction, but it produces strength.

The good news is that difficult conversations don't have to be destructive. When handled with humility, love, and intentionality, they can become some of the most meaningful and strengthening moments in a marriage. Ephesians 4:15 encourages believers to *"speak the truth in love,"* showing us that honesty and grace are meant to walk hand in hand.

In this chapter, we will explore some of the common issues couples inevitably face and why they so often lead to tension. More importantly, we will focus on practical, faith-centered ways to work through these conversations, making them less intimidating, more productive, and ultimately more unifying. Rather than something to fear, difficult conversations can become tools God uses to deepen understanding, build trust, and strengthen the bond between husband and wife.

Preparing Your Heart Before a Tough Conversation

When a tough conversation in marriage becomes inevitable, the most important preparation often has little to do with *what* we are going to say and everything to do with the *condition of our hearts before we say it*. Many conversations go poorly not because the issue is unimportant, but because we step into the discussion already defensive, frustrated, or determined to win an argument rather than protect the relationship. Preparation begins internally, aligning our motives, emotions, and posture before we ever open our mouths.

Scripture repeatedly emphasizes the heart as the source of our words and actions. Proverbs 4:23 reminds us, *"Above all else, guard your heart, for everything you do flows from it."* Before addressing a difficult issue, taking time to pray, reflect, and invite God into the process helps shift our focus from self-protection to unity. Prayer reorients us from *"How do I prove my point?"* to *"How can I love my spouse well in this moment?"*

Another key step is examining our motives. Psalm 139:23–24 says, *"Search me, God, and know my heart... see if there is any offensive way in me."* Asking God to reveal pride, resentment, or fear allows us to enter the conversation with humility rather than accusation. James 1:19 further instructs us to be *"quick to listen, slow to speak, and slow to become angry."* This mindset alone can dramatically change the tone and outcome of a conversation.

From a practical standpoint, emotional regulation is essential. Pausing before the conversation to calm your body and mind, through deep breathing, journaling, or even a short walk, can prevent emotional flooding that leads to harsh words or shutdown. Research in communication and relationship psychology consistently shows that people communicate more effectively when they are calm and feel emotionally safe.

Clarifying your goal is another powerful step. Ask yourself: *What is the outcome I'm hoping for?* A healthy goal is not winning the argument but strengthening understanding and connection. Approaching the conversation with curiosity rather than certainty opens space for dialogue instead of debate. Using "I" statements instead of "you" accusations helps keep the conversation focused on feelings and needs rather than blame.

Timing also matters. Choosing a moment when both spouses are rested, present, and not distracted increases the likelihood of a positive outcome. Difficult conversations rarely go well when one or both partners are tired, hungry, or stressed. Respecting timing is a way to honor your spouse and your relationship.

Creating a Win-Win Outcome

Biblically and practically, success in a difficult conversation is not measured by who is right, but by whether the relationship is strengthened. Philippians 2:3–4 urges believers to *"do nothing out of selfish ambition or vain conceit. Rather, in humility value others above yourselves."* This doesn't mean ignoring your needs; it means valuing unity over ego.

A helpful non-biblical principle aligns closely with this truth: *partners, not opponents.* When couples view the issue as the enemy, rather than each other, they are more likely to collaborate on solutions. Reassuring your spouse of your commitment and love at the beginning of the conversation can lower defenses and set a cooperative tone.

Ultimately, preparing your heart allows both spouses to "win" because the goal becomes mutual understanding, emotional safety, and forward progress. When truth is spoken with love, and when preparation replaces reaction, tough conversations can produce healing rather than harm. These moments, though uncomfortable, can become opportunities for growth, deeper intimacy, and a stronger, more Christ-centered marriage.

The Power of Gentle Confrontation

When conflict arises in marriage, the way confrontation is handled often determines whether the conversation leads to healing or harm. Scripture is clear that gentleness is not weakness but a powerful force for de-escalation and restoration. Proverbs 15:1 reminds us that *"a gentle answer turns away wrath, but a harsh word stirs up anger."* This principle speaks directly to the emotional dynamics of conflict: intensity invites resistance, while gentleness invites openness. When a spouse comes into a conversation highly charged, angry, or aggressive, the other person's nervous system immediately shifts into defense mode. Words are filtered through fear rather than understanding, and the conflict escalates. In contrast, gentle confrontation lowers defenses and creates a sense of emotional safety, which is essential for any productive resolution.

In marriage, gentle confrontation means addressing real issues honestly, but doing so with humility, patience, and love. Ephesians 4:15 calls believers to *"speak the truth in love,"* showing that truth and gentleness are not opposites, they are partners. This kind of confrontation does not ignore problems or minimize feelings; instead, it communicates, "You matter more to me than being right." James 1:19 reinforces this posture by urging us to be *"quick to listen, slow to speak, and slow to anger."* When couples follow this biblical rhythm, conversations shift from emotional combat to meaningful dialogue.

A practical example of this can be seen in moments between Michelle and me. Imagine a situation where I come into a conversation extremely upset, my voice is raised, my frustration is obvious, and I am emotionally flooded. If Michelle were to match my intensity or respond defensively, the tension would almost certainly escalate. I would feel challenged rather than understood, and the issue would quickly turn into a battle over tone and attitude instead of the actual problem. However, when Michelle responds gently, acknowledging my frustration and expressing a desire to understand, it changes the entire atmosphere. A calm response like, *"I can see how upset you are, and I really want to understand what's going on,"* immediately lowers my defenses. Her gentleness does not excuse my anger, but it disarms it. I begin to calm down, my heart softens, and I can communicate more clearly and listen more openly. What could have become destructive instead becomes an opportunity for connection and resolution.

This dynamic is not just biblical; it is strongly supported by relationship research. Studies consistently show that aggressive or hostile communication styles are linked to lower marital satisfaction and higher levels of unresolved conflict. In contrast, cooperative and validating communication, where one partner responds with calmness and empathy, leads to better problem-solving and emotional closeness. Research also indicates that poor communication is cited by an overwhelming majority of dissatisfied couples as a primary contributor to marital distress, while couples who learn healthier communication and conflict-resolution skills report significantly improved satisfaction. These findings reinforce what Scripture has taught all along: how we speak matters as much as what we say.

Highly charged, forceful confrontation may feel productive in the moment, but it often causes more destruction than good. It leaves emotional bruises, reinforces defensiveness, and can create long-term patterns of fear or withdrawal. Gentle confrontation, on the other hand, promotes:

- De-escalation rather than escalation

- Emotional safety instead of defensiveness

- Collaboration instead of competition

- Resolution that strengthens the relationship rather than weakening it

Ultimately, gentle confrontation reflects the heart of Christ. Philippians 2:3–4 calls us to *"act in humility, valuing others above ourselves."* In marriage, this means choosing connection over control and understanding over intensity. When one spouse responds gently in the face of anger,

it can calm emotions, reset the tone, and open the door to a solution that honors both people. Gentleness does not avoid truth, it carries truth in a way that heals, restores, and leads to lasting unity.

Avoiding Avoidance – Why Silence Can Be Destructive

The next issue we need to address in conflict is **avoidance**, because while many couples fear confrontation, silence can be just as damaging, sometimes more so. In many marriages, one spouse will say, *"My spouse never communicates. They just shut down and won't talk."* This pattern can feel confusing and deeply frustrating, especially to the partner who wants resolution. What's important to understand is that **silence is not the absence of communication, it is communication**. When a spouse avoids conversation, withdraws emotionally, or refuses to engage, they are still sending a message, even if no words are spoken.

When conflict is met with silence, several unspoken messages are often communicated, whether intentionally or not. Silence can imply, *"This issue isn't important enough to talk about,"* or *"Your feelings don't matter to me right now,"* or *"I don't want to deal with this, so I'm shutting you out."* Over time, this can feel dismissive or rejecting to the other spouse. Even if the silent partner's intent is self-protection or avoiding escalation, the impact is often hurt, loneliness, and emotional distance. Proverbs 18:1 warns that withdrawing oneself leads to broken judgment and isolation, reinforcing the idea that pulling away does not produce wisdom or peace in relationships.

Research strongly supports the idea that avoidance and emotional shutdown are harmful to marriages. Relationship researcher John Gottman identifies **stonewalling** — withdrawing, shutting down, or refusing to engage — as one of the "Four Horsemen" that predict marital breakdown. Studies have shown that chronic avoidance during conflict is linked to lower marital satisfaction, increased resentment, and unresolved issues that resurface repeatedly. Some research suggests that couples who rely heavily on avoidance strategies experience higher stress levels and less emotional intimacy over time, because problems are never truly addressed, only postponed.

Avoidance does not make conflict disappear; it simply drives it underground. Unresolved issues don't fade away, they accumulate. When communication stops, assumptions take over. The spouse who wants to talk may begin to feel unheard, unvalued, or emotionally abandoned,

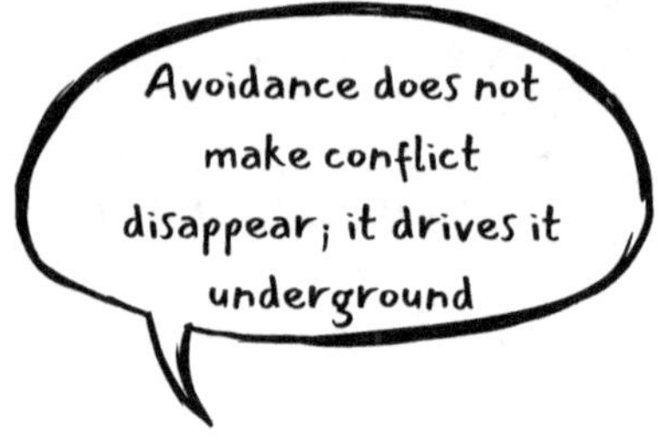

while the silent spouse may feel overwhelmed, unsafe, or ill-equipped to express themselves. This cycle creates a growing gap between partners, where neither feels fully understood. Ecclesiastes 3 reminds us there is *"a time to keep silent and a time to speak."* In marriage, conflict resolution almost always requires speaking at the right time rather than permanent withdrawal.

Healthy marriages require a willingness to engage, even when it's uncomfortable. Avoidance may feel like peace, but it is often a false peace that sacrifices connection for temporary relief. Ephesians 4:26 encourages couples to deal with conflict promptly and intentionally, reminding us not to let unresolved issues linger. Openness and communication are not about arguing more, but about creating space to understand, heal, and move forward together.

Helping a silent partner open up must be done carefully and gently, without turning the conversation into another conflict. The goal is safety, not pressure. Approaching them calmly, choosing the right timing, and expressing curiosity rather than accusation can make a significant difference. Statements like, *"I'm not trying to fight, I just want to understand you,"* or *"Your thoughts matter to me, and I'd really like to hear them when you're ready,"* invite engagement without demand. Validating their feelings, especially if silence is rooted in fear, past experiences, or emotional overload, can help lower their defenses.

Creating a healthy path forward often means agreeing on shared expectations for communication. This might include allowing time to cool down while committing to return to the conversation later, or setting boundaries that ensure issues are addressed respectfully rather than avoided indefinitely. When both spouses understand that communication is about partnership, not punishment, it becomes easier to engage. Ultimately, conflict handled with openness, patience, and grace strengthens trust and deepens intimacy. Silence may feel safer in the moment, but honest, loving communication is what truly builds a resilient and healthy marriage.

How to Express Needs Without Demanding Change

When we sit down to mentor hurting couples in crisis, one pattern shows up almost every time. In those first conversations, couples pour out everything that's gone wrong in the relationship. They describe the pain, the disappointment, the arguments, and the long list of things they've already tried to "fix" the marriage. By the time they finish, many of them sound exhausted and almost ready to end the relationship altogether. Then we ask a simple but revealing question: *"What is it you would like us to help you accomplish during this time of mentorship?"* And almost without fail, the answer comes back in one form or another: *"I just need you to change them."*

On the surface, it's almost comical, if it weren't so painfully real. What that response reveals is something deeply human. In our everyday world, selfishness comes naturally to all of us. When things go wrong, it's far easier to point the finger outward than to look inward. Blame feels safer than responsibility. We instinctively focus on what our spouse is doing wrong, how *they* need to grow, how *they* need to stop, start, or change in order for the marriage to improve. Rarely do we come into those conversations asking, "What needs to change in me?"

This mindset keeps couples stuck. As long as the goal is to fix or change the other person, true healing can't begin. Scripture reminds us that transformation starts in the heart, not in controlling someone else (Romans 12:2). Healthy mentorship gently redirects couples away from blame and toward personal ownership, helping each spouse see that while they cannot change their partner, they *can* choose humility, repentance, forgiveness, and growth. Real change in a marriage almost always begins when both people stop pointing fingers and start allowing God to do His refining work in their own hearts first.

To move toward healing, couples have to intentionally step out of the *"change them"* mindset and learn a healthier way to communicate what they need. There is an important distinction here. Yes, some things absolutely need to change, especially sinful, destructive, or unhealthy behaviors that are tearing a marriage apart, such as dishonesty, abuse, addiction, or ongoing disrespect. Addressing those behaviors is necessary for safety, trust, and restoration. But that is very different from trying to change a spouse's **personality**.

When we marry, we are joining our lives with someone who is wired differently than we are. God created each of us with unique temperaments, communication styles, emotional responses, and ways of processing the world. It is never our role to reshape our spouse into a version of ourselves or into who we *wish* they were.

When a spouse consistently tries to change the other's personality, the long-term effects are damaging. Over time, it often breeds resentment because the spouse being "fixed" begins to feel like they are never enough. They can feel criticized rather than cherished, corrected rather than accepted. This creates emotional distance and defensiveness, slowly eroding trust. Instead of feeling safe in the relationship, they may start walking on eggshells, withholding parts of themselves, or shutting down altogether. It can also damage intimacy, because vulnerability requires acceptance. When someone feels they are loved only if they change who they are, the bond weakens, and the marriage shifts from partnership to power struggle.

A healthier path forward is learning to express needs without demanding change, communicating in ways that invite connection rather than resistance. One proven way to do this is by taking ownership of our feelings and experiences. Using "I" statements instead of "you" accusations help lower defenses. For example, saying, *"I feel disconnected when we don't talk in the evenings, and I really need some intentional time with you,"* is far more effective than, *"You never talk to me, and you need to change."* This approach shares a need without attacking character.

Another powerful practice is focusing on the impact rather than the flaw. Explaining how a behavior affects you emotionally helps your spouse understand your heart, not just your frustration. Listening is equally important. When both spouses feel heard and validated, even when they don't fully agree, the emotional bond strengthens. Research consistently shows that couples who practice empathy, validation, and curiosity toward one another experience greater marital satisfaction and resilience during conflict.

It is also helpful to frame needs as **invitations** rather than ultimatums. Inviting your spouse into a solution communicates respect and teamwork: *"Can we find a rhythm that works for both of us?"* rather than *"This has to change."* Expressing appreciation for what your spouse already does well further reinforces safety and goodwill. Gratitude softens difficult conversations and reminds both people that they are on the same side.

Let's take a small look at the last option using an example with my wife, Michelle, and me.

Imagine a season where life has been busy, and Michelle begins to feel emotionally disconnected because we haven't been spending much intentional time talking. Her need for connection is real and valid, but how she communicates that need will determine the direction of the conversation and, ultimately, the outcome in our marriage.

If Michelle approaches me from an ultimatum or demand-for-change posture, the conversation might sound like this: *"You never talk to me anymore. You're always distracted or busy, and I'm tired of feeling ignored. You need to change and start prioritizing me."* Even though her desire for connection is legitimate, the way she delivers it immediately puts me on the defensive. Instead of hearing her heart, I hear an accusation. My focus shifts from understanding her need to protecting myself. I may shut down, argue back, or minimize the issue altogether. Michelle then feels even more unheard and frustrated when the conversation escalates or goes nowhere. We both walk away feeling misunderstood and disconnected, and the original goal of closeness is completely lost. Over time, this pattern only increases resentment and emotional distance.

Now consider how the same need can be expressed from an invitation stance. Michelle might come to me and say, *"Daniel, I want to share something with you. Lately, I've been feeling disconnected, and I really miss our conversations. Talking with you helps me feel close and secure. Could we look at our schedules and find a way to create some intentional time together?"* In this approach, she owns her feelings without attacking my character. Instead of demanding change, she invites me into the solution. I don't feel accused; I feel wanted. I'm much more likely to respond with empathy and say something like, *"I didn't realize you were feeling that way. I don't want you to feel disconnected. Let's figure something out together."* The conversation naturally moves toward teamwork and problem-solving rather than blame.

The difference between these two outcomes isn't the need itself, it's the posture. An ultimatum creates resistance, while an invitation creates safety. When Michelle invites me into the conversation instead of trying to change me, she communicates, *"I want you, not a different version of you."* That kind of approach honors our differences, preserves dignity, and strengthens trust. In a marriage, ultimatums push spouses apart, but invitations draw them together. When needs are expressed with humility, ownership, and grace, real change often happens, not because it was demanded, but because love made room for it.

Expressing needs without demanding change shifts the marriage from control to connection. It creates an environment where growth happens naturally, not forcefully. When spouses feel accepted, valued, and respected as God created them, they are far more willing to grow, adjust, and sacrifice, not out of pressure, but out of love.

Handling Emotionally Charged Topics with Wisdom

One last critical topic for this chapter is learning to use **wisdom** in emotionally charged moments. Conflict is rarely just about the issue on the surface; it is often fueled by fear, hurt, feeling misunderstood, or feeling attacked. Using myself as an example, I am what you would call an *escalator* in heated moments. When I feel attacked or misunderstood, my natural tendency is to raise my voice, use stronger language, and push harder to be heard. For people with this kind of conflict personality, escalation often feels like self-protection. It is an instinctive response driven by the belief that if we speak louder, firmer, or stronger, we will finally be understood. Unfortunately, while escalation may feel justified in the moment, it almost always escalates the conflict itself rather than resolving it.

People who respond this way are often deeply invested in clarity, justice, or accurate representation. When those things feel threatened, emotions surge, and the body goes into a defensive mode. In those moments, logic gives way to reaction, and tone becomes sharper even if the heart's

desire is resolution. This is exactly where wisdom must step in. Scripture reminds us that wisdom is not simply knowing what is right but choosing the right response at the right time. *"The wisdom from above is first pure, then peaceable, gentle, open to reason, full of mercy and good fruits"* (James 3:17). Wisdom slows us down when everything in us wants to speed up.

Bringing God into emotionally charged conversations starts with pausing the reaction and acknowledging His presence. Even a silent prayer in the moment, *"Lord, guard my words and my tone"*, can realign the heart. Proverbs 16:23 tells us that *"the heart of the wise makes his speech judicious and adds persuasiveness to his lips."* That means wisdom begins internally before it ever comes out verbally. Choosing to pause, breathe, and submit our emotions to God shifts the atmosphere of the conversation from confrontation to discernment.

Another biblical example of wisdom in heated moments is found in Proverbs 15:1: *"A soft answer turns away wrath, but a harsh word stirs up anger."* For an escalator, this verse is deeply counterintuitive. Everything in the flesh wants to respond with intensity, yet God's wisdom calls for gentleness. When an escalator chooses a softer tone instead of a louder one, it interrupts the cycle of conflict. The emotional temperature in the room begins to drop, making space for understanding instead of further damage.

Ecclesiastes 7:9 offers another layer of wisdom: *"Be not quick in your spirit to become angry, for anger lodges in the heart of fools."* This doesn't mean anger itself is sinful, but that unchecked, rapid anger leads to foolish outcomes. Wisdom teaches us to recognize when emotions are running high and to delay the conversation if needed. Saying something like, *"I want to talk about this, but I need a moment to calm my heart, so I don't say something I'll regret,"* is not avoidance — it is spiritual maturity. It invites God into the process by prioritizing righteousness over being right.

Jesus Himself models this kind of wisdom. When He was falsely accused, mocked, and misunderstood, Scripture tells us He often remained silent or responded with measured words (Isaiah 53:7; Matthew 26:62–63). His restraint was not weakness; it was strength under control. By entrusting Himself to the Father, Jesus showed that wisdom sometimes speaks less, not more. When we follow His example in marriage, we learn that we don't have to win the argument to protect our hearts or our dignity, God does that for us.

When wisdom is invited into emotionally charged moments, everything about the outcome changes. Escalation gives way to self-control, defensiveness gives way to humility, and chaos gives way to peace. Instead of walking away with regret and deeper wounds, couples walk away with understanding, safety, and often a deeper connection than before. Bringing God into the conversation doesn't remove emotion, but it redeems it, turning moments that could divide a marriage into opportunities for growth, healing, and grace.

Chapter Eight

Speaking Love in Your Spouses Language

Biblical Foundation: 1 Corinthians 13:1-7, John 13:34

Communication in marriage often breaks down not because spouses don't love each other, but because they are speaking different emotional languages. One spouse may feel they are expressing care clearly, while the other feels unheard, unseen, or unloved. The problem isn't usually effort — it's translation.

Just as people express love in different ways, they also *receive* love differently through communication. A kind intention can land as indifference. Honest feedback can sound like rejection. Silence can feel like peace to one spouse and abandonment to the other. When we fail to recognize how our spouse experiences love through words, tone, timing, and attention, even well-meaning conversations can create distance rather than connection.

Scripture reminds us that love must be expressed with understanding. *"Let each of you look not only to his own interests, but also to the interests of others"* (Philippians 2:4). In marriage, that means learning how your spouse feels valued, respected, and emotionally safe, not how *you* would want to be treated, but how *they* receive love best.

In this chapter, we will explore how identifying your spouse's love language within communication can transform everyday conversations. When you learn to speak in ways your spouse's heart understands, conflict softens, trust deepens, and communication becomes a tool for unity rather than division.

Identifying Your Spouse's Love Language in Communication

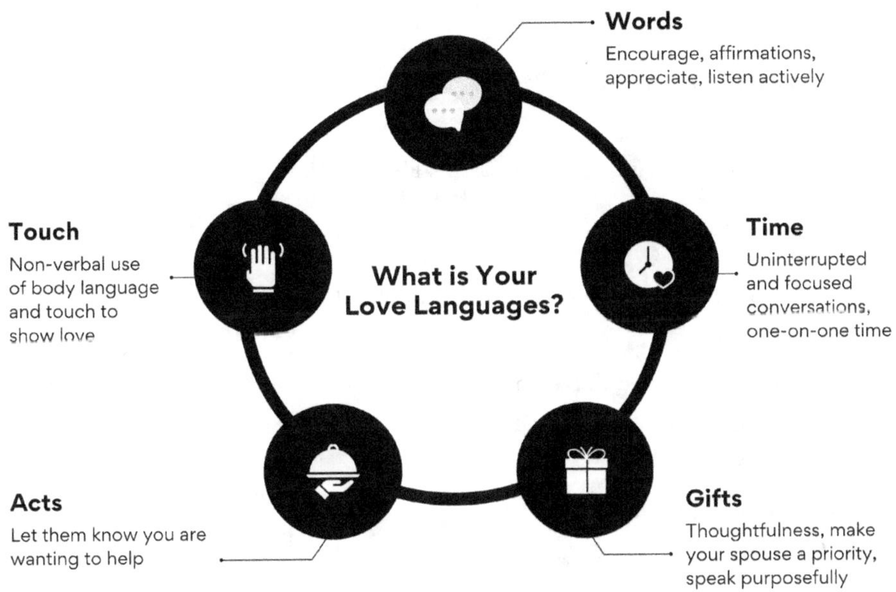

Understanding your spouse's love language means recognizing *how they feel most valued, affirmed, and emotionally safe,* especially during conversation. It's not just about what you say, but **how**, **when**, and **why** you say it. Each person filters words through a different emotional lens, shaped by personality, upbringing, and past experiences. When that lens is ignored, even loving intentions can feel hurtful.

For example, a spouse whose primary love language is **Words of Affirmation** often needs verbal reassurance, encouragement, and acknowledgment to feel secure. Silence or blunt communication may feel dismissive, even if no harm is intended. On the other hand, a spouse whose love language is **Acts of Service** may prioritize problem-solving and action over emotional processing. To them, fixing the issue *is* the expression of love.

When couples fail to understand these differences, communication can quickly turn frustrating. One spouse feels unappreciated, while the other feels misunderstood. The result is not a lack of love, but a lack of alignment.

Let's take a look at an example of a couple struggling through a conversation, with each person speaking a different love language.

Sarah's primary love language is *Words of Affirmation*. She needs verbal support and empathy.

Mark's primary love language is *Acts of Service*. He shows love by solving problems.

Sarah:

"I had such a hard day today. I feel like I can't do anything right at work."

Mark:

"Well, maybe you just need to be more organized. You've been staying up too late and that probably doesn't help."

Sarah (hurt):

"So, you think this is my fault?"

Mark (confused):

"No, I'm just trying to help. I'm giving you a solution."

Sarah:

"I didn't ask for a solution. I just needed you to understand how overwhelmed I feel."

Mark (defensive):

"I *am* trying to help. What do you want me to do, sit there and say nothing?"

In this exchange, Mark believes he is loving Sarah by offering a fix. In his mind, action equals care. But Sarah hears criticism where she needs compassion. Because Mark doesn't recognize that Sarah receives love through *affirming words*, his attempt to help actually deepens the hurt.

Neither spouse is wrong. They are speaking different love languages.

When spouses learn to understand each other's love language in communication, conversations shift. Empathy replaces defensiveness. Validation comes before solutions. Love is not just intended, it is *felt*.

Understanding your spouse's love language doesn't mean abandoning your own communication style. It means choosing to love them in a way their heart can receive.

Here are the **five love languages** and what each one typically *need from their spouse in conversation* to feel loved, safe, and connected. (People can have more than one strong language, and love languages don't excuse sin or harshness — they help you love with understanding.)

1. Words of Affirmation

What it is: Love is felt through **spoken (or written) encouragement, appreciation, reassurance, and respect**.

What this love language requires in healthy conversation:

- **Start with warmth before critique.** "I love you... I'm with you... We'll figure this out."

- **Be specific with praise.** "I appreciate how you handled bedtime tonight."

- **Use a gentle tone.** Tone matters as much as content.

- **Repair quickly after conflict.** "I'm sorry. I shouldn't have said that. You matter to me."

- **Avoid sarcasm, teasing jabs, and silent treatment.** Those land as rejection.

In conflict, they need: validation + reassurance before solutions.
Sounds like: "That makes sense. I can see why you'd feel that. I'm here."

2. Acts of Service

What it is: Love is felt when a spouse **reduces burdens** through helpful action, especially practical follow-through.

What this love language requires in healthy conversation:

- **Don't just empathize — partner with a plan.** "What can I take off your plate this week?"

- **Follow through on what you say.** Promises without action feel empty.

- **Communicate clearly and concretely.** Vague talk can feel like spinning wheels.

- **Ask "What would help?" instead of assuming.**

- **Don't criticize their efforts.** If you correct every detail, they'll stop trying.

In conflict, they need: clarity + actionable next steps.
Sounds like: "Okay, what's one thing I can do today to make this better?"

3. Quality Time

What it is: Love is felt through **focused attention and shared presence** — not just being in the same room.

What this love language requires in healthy conversation:

- **Undivided attention.** Phones down, TV off, eye contact.

- **Unhurried listening.** They need time to land the plane, don't rush them.

- **Curiosity questions.** "Tell me more... what did that feel like?"

- **Consistent check-ins.** Connection isn't occasional; it's regular.

- **Don't "half-listen."** Multitasking often reads as "you don't matter."

In conflict, they need: time + presence more than a quick resolution.
Sounds like: "Let's sit down tonight and talk this through with no distractions."

4. Physical Touch

What it is: Love is felt through **appropriate affection** — handholding, hugs, cuddling, a comforting touch, and yes, sexual intimacy in marriage.

What this love language requires in healthy conversation:

- **Warmth before words.** Touch can lower defensiveness and increase safety.

- **Affection that isn't always a "transaction."** Not every touch should feel like it leads to sex.

- **Gentle repair after disagreement.** A hand on the shoulder, a hug, sitting close.

- **Respect boundaries and timing.** Touch must be safe and welcomed.

- **Don't weaponize withdrawal.** Withholding affection to punish creates insecurity.

In conflict, they need: reassurance + closeness (when appropriate).
Sounds like: "Can I hold your hand while we talk? I'm not against you."

5. Receiving Gifts

What it is: Love is felt through **thoughtfulness made tangible** — a gift is a symbol of being remembered and valued (not a price tag).

What this love language requires in healthy conversation:

- **Remember what matters to them.** Their likes, burdens, big days, and stress points.

- **Mark moments.** A note, a coffee, a small "I saw this and thought of you."

- **Don't mock it as materialism.** For them, it means not money.

- **Use "tokens of repair."** A sincere note or small, thoughtful gesture can soften hearts.

- **Consistency matters.** Forgetting anniversaries/birthdays can feel like being forgotten.

In conflict, they need: evidence of thought + intentional pursuit.
Sounds like: "I've been thinking about what you said. I wrote you a note."

What a Healthy Conversation Looks Like When You Know Their Love Language

A simple pattern that works across all five:

1. **Connect** (love language)

2. **Clarify** (what they mean)

3. **Care** (validate feelings)

4. **Collaborate** (next step)

Example:

- **Words:** "I'm grateful for you."

- **Time:** "Let's talk with no distractions."

- **Service:** "What would help most right now?"

- **Touch:** "Can I sit close while we work this out?"

- **Gifts:** "I brought you something small—because you matter."

Identifying your spouse's love language begins with paying attention, not to what *you* prefer, but to what *they* consistently respond to. Notice what lifts their spirit, what wounds them most deeply, and what they often ask for during moments of stress or conflict. Pay attention to how they express love to you, because people often give what they most want to receive. Listen for repeated phrases like, "I just need you to listen," "I wish you'd help more," or "You never say anything nice anymore." Those statements are clues, not complaints.

You can also identify your spouse's love language by observing what they miss when it's absent and what restores connection when it's offered. The goal is not to label your spouse, but to understand them. When you learn to recognize the language their heart speaks, you move from guessing to loving intentionally, and communication becomes an act of care, not conflict.

For a full in-depth study of these love languages, visit www.5lovelanguages.com. Dr. Gary Chapman has written and produced numerous resources on understanding each other through the love languages and navigating them in your conversations and marriage. There is also a quiz you can take at that website to see which language you and your spouse tend to navigate toward.

Words That Build Trust vs. Words That Create Distance

I once heard a statement that has always stuck with me: **"Trust is earned in drops and lost in buckets."** It captures a hard but important truth about marriage.

In a healthy marriage, trust is the emotional safety net that allows two people to be fully known without fear. It's what gives words their weight and intentions their credibility. When trust is strong, a careless comment can be brushed off, a misunderstanding can be clarified, and conflict doesn't threaten the foundation. But when trust is damaged, even small words can feel heavy, suspicious, or threatening.

Trust is often lost in "buckets" because it usually isn't destroyed by one dramatic moment, but by repeated patterns — dismissive tones, broken promises, sarcasm, criticism, or words spoken without care. A spouse may not remember every individual comment, but they remember how those words made them feel: **unseen, unsafe,** or **unvalued**. Over time, those moments accumulate, and the emotional reserve of trust drains quickly.

Words are especially powerful because they reveal what we believe about our spouse. A harsh comment, a public criticism, or a careless joke can signal, *I don't respect you,* even if that was never the intention. When that happens, trust erodes, and distance grows. A spouse may begin to guard their heart, filter what they share, or stop bringing concerns altogether, not to punish, but to protect themselves. Silence replaces vulnerability. Defensiveness replaces openness. What was once a partnership translates into a cautious coexistence.

Regaining trust, however, is slow and deliberate — one drop at a time. It is rebuilt through consistent humility, sincere repentance, and changed behavior. Apologies matter, but what restores trust most is follow-through: **gentler words, kept commitments**, and a **noticeable effort to communicate with grace**. Each respectful conversation, each moment of listening without defensiveness, adds a small drop back into the bucket.

In marriage, words are never neutral. They either build safety or create space. When we speak without wisdom, we don't just hurt feelings; we weaken trust. But when we choose words that are honest, kind, and measured, we create an environment where trust can grow, intimacy can deepen, and communication can once again draw two hearts closer rather than push them apart.

6 Steps to Rebuilding Trust

Rebuilding trust after it has been broken is one of the most difficult—and most meaningful—works a couple can undertake

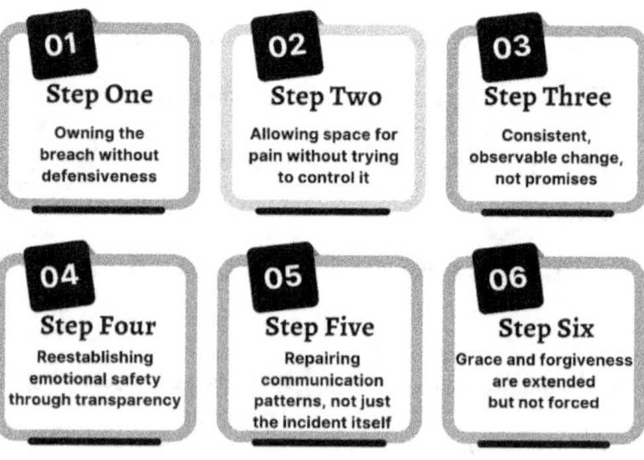

Rebuilding trust after it has been broken is one of the most difficult, and most meaningful, works a couple can undertake. Trust is not restored by time alone or by simply "moving on." It is rebuilt through intentional, consistent, and humble actions that demonstrate safety over time. The goal is not just to return to how things were, but to create a relationship that is more honest, more secure, and more resilient than before.

The first essential step in rebuilding trust is **owning the breach without defensiveness**. The spouse who caused the harm must take full responsibility for their words or actions without minimizing the impact, shifting blame, or rushing the healing process. Statements like "I didn't mean it that way" or "You're too sensitive" further damage trust by invalidating the hurt. Healing begins when the injured spouse feels heard and understood. Genuine ownership sounds like, "I see how my words hurt you, and I take responsibility for that."

The second step is **allowing space for pain without trying to control it**. When trust is broken, the wounded spouse often needs time to process emotions such as sadness, anger, fear, or confusion. These emotions are not obstacles to healing; they are part of it. Pressuring a spouse to "get over it" or setting timelines for forgiveness can deepen the wound. A safe space is rebuilt when the hurting spouse is allowed to grieve openly, and the other spouse remains present, patient, and compassionate.

Third, trust is restored through **consistent, observable change**, not promises. Apologies matter, but changed behavior is what rebuilds credibility. This means intentionally altering the patterns that caused the breach — speaking more gently, keeping commitments, choosing honesty even when it's uncomfortable, and responding differently in moments of tension. Over time, consistency reassures the wounded spouse that the harm is not likely to be repeated. Each repeated choice to act differently adds another "drop" back into the bucket of trust.

Another critical step is **reestablishing emotional safety through transparency**. Transparency means there are no hidden motives, guarded conversations, or unexplained behaviors. The spouse rebuilding trust may need to over-communicate for a season — not to be controlled, but to demonstrate openness. Transparency communicates, "You don't have to wonder where I stand anymore." When questions are answered calmly and truthfully, anxiety decreases, and security slowly returns.

Rebuilding trust also requires **repairing communication patterns**, not just addressing the incident itself. Couples must learn to talk about hard things without attacking, withdrawing, or escalating. This includes learning to listen without interrupting, to validate without agreeing, and to express concerns without contempt. Healthy communication creates predictability, and predictability is a cornerstone of trust. When a spouse knows how conflict will be handled, fear is reduced.

Finally, trust is fully restored when **grace and forgiveness are extended but not forced**. Forgiveness is a choice to release resentment, not a denial of pain or a shortcut around accountability. It often comes in stages and may need to be reaffirmed over time. As forgiveness grows and consistent safety is demonstrated, the relationship gradually becomes a safe space again — one where vulnerability is possible, honesty is welcomed, and love is expressed without fear.

Rebuilding trust is slow, but it is not impossible. When both spouses commit to humility, consistency, and compassion, what was once broken can be restored, not by ignoring the damage, but by faithfully rebuilding, one careful step at a time.

Using Encouragement as a Regular Communication Practice

Encouragement is one of the most overlooked yet powerful communication practices in a marriage. At its core, encouragement means putting courage into your spouse through your words, tone, and presence. It is not flattery, exaggeration, or shallow positivity, but a steady commitment to speak life, hope, and truth — even when circumstances are hard. When encouragement becomes regular rather than occasional, it begins to shape the emotional climate of the relationship. Words spoken consistently carry far more weight than words spoken sporadically. Over time, they influence how safe a spouse feels, how confident they grow, and how willing they are to engage rather than withdraw.

The **absence of encouragement** often speaks louder than intentional silence. When affirmation, gratitude, and recognition are missing, many spouses quietly assume disapproval or indifference. Encouragement, on the other hand, communicates value. It says, "I see you. I appreciate you. You matter to me." These messages do not require grand gestures or perfectly crafted statements; they are most powerful when expressed in everyday moments, acknowledging effort, recognizing growth, and affirming character. A marriage filled with encouragement becomes a place where both spouses feel supported rather than scrutinized.

Regular encouragement also creates the emotional safety necessary for healthy conversations, especially difficult ones. Correction without encouragement often feels like rejection, causing defensiveness and distance. Encouragement does not ignore problems or pretend weaknesses do not exist; instead, it establishes a foundation of trust that allows hard conversations to be heard without fear. When a spouse knows they are valued, correction feels like care rather than condemnation. Encouragement assures them that the relationship itself is not in question, even when an issue arises.

Another key to practicing encouragement well is understanding how your spouse receives it. Encouragement must be felt, not just intended. For some, words of affirmation are essential; for others, encouragement is communicated through time, service, physical affection, or thoughtful actions. When encouragement is offered in a way that aligns with your spouse's emotional needs, it becomes deeply impactful. When it misses those needs, it can feel distant or incomplete, even when the heart behind it is sincere.

Encouragement is most transformative when it remains present during conflict. In moments of tension, it reminds both spouses that they are on the same team. Speaking respectfully, reassurance, and commitment during disagreement prevent communication from becoming destructive. Statements that affirm love and unity, even while expressing frustration, help preserve connection and keep conflict from eroding trust. Over time, this practice strengthens the marriage by replacing fear and defensiveness with confidence and security.

When encouragement becomes a regular rhythm in communication, it shapes the long-term health of the relationship. Encouraged spouses are more likely to grow, engage, and take emotional risks. Discouraged spouses tend to shut down, retreat, or protect themselves. The words spoken repeatedly in a marriage become the emotional legacy left behind. A home marked by encouragement becomes a place of refuge, growth, and resilience, where communication no longer tears down but consistently builds up.

Scripture reminds us that our words are never neutral. Proverbs tell us that *"death and life are in the power of the tongue,"* and Paul exhorts us in Ephesians 4:29 to *"speak only what is helpful for building others up according to their needs."* In other words, encouragement is not optional — it is a biblical responsibility. Our words are meant to strengthen, heal, and impart grace, especially to the person we are closest to. When encouragement becomes a regular practice, communication shifts from merely exchanging information to actively cultivating safety, trust, and growth. A marriage that is rich in encouragement becomes a place where both spouses are reminded daily that they are valued, capable, and not alone.

Most marriages don't fall apart because one spouse forgot to say something brilliant; they suffer because one spouse forgot to say something kind. Encouragement doesn't require eloquence or a seminary degree. It simply requires intention. You don't need to preach a sermon every morning, sometimes "thank you," "I see you," or "I'm proud of you" will do just fine. Your spouse doesn't need a motivational speaker; they need a partner who chooses life-giving words more often than sighs, sarcasm, or silence. When encouragement becomes your default language, communication stops feeling like a minefield and starts feeling like home, and that's a place both of you actually want to stay.

Emotional Safety: Creating a Judgment-Free Environment

Emotional safety is the foundation of healthy communication. Without it, even the best intentions are filtered through fear, defensiveness, or silence. Emotional safety exists when a person knows they can speak honestly without being mocked, dismissed, punished, or emotionally abandoned. It is not the absence of disagreement, but the presence of respect. In a judgment-free environment, a spouse is allowed to be human — to be imperfect, emotional, unsure, or even wrong — without feeling exposed or unsafe.

When emotional safety is missing, communication begins to shut down. Words become guarded, feelings are withheld, and conversations stay shallow because vulnerability feels risky. Over time, this creates distance in the relationship. One spouse may stop sharing altogether, not because they have nothing to say, but because experience has taught them that honesty leads to criticism, escalation, or shame. Emotional safety is what allows truth to be spoken without fear of relational damage.

Many couples unintentionally break emotional safety through small, repeated behaviors rather than major betrayals. Eyerolling, sarcastic remarks, interrupting, or dismissive tones communicate contempt even when the words themselves seem harmless. Phrases like "you're too sensitive," "you always do this," or "that's not a big deal" send the message that feelings are not welcome here. Even bringing up past mistakes during a disagreement can make a spouse feel exposed and judged. When emotional reactions are used as weapons later, vulnerability becomes a liability instead of a bridge.

Judgment plays a central role in shutting people down emotionally. Judgment does not always sound harsh or cruel; often, it disguises itself as honesty or concern. Statements meant to "fix" a spouse can feel like verdicts rather than support. Judgment communicates that acceptance is conditional and that emotional expression will be evaluated instead of received. Over time, this teaches a spouse to filter their thoughts before speaking — or to stop speaking altogether. Most people are not afraid of being wrong; they are afraid of being shamed.

Creating a judgment-free environment begins with curiosity. Curiosity invites understanding instead of defensiveness. Asking questions like "Can you help me understand how that felt?" or "What was going through your mind?" keeps the conversation open and communicates care. **Curiosity** slows reactions and shifts the goal from winning an argument to learning your spouse's heart. When curiosity leads, safety follows.

Validation is another essential component of emotional safety. Validation does not mean agreement; it means acknowledgment. Saying "I can see why that hurt you" or "That makes sense from your perspective" allows a spouse to feel heard before correction or resolution begins. Many conversations escalate not because someone is wrong, but because someone feels unseen. Validation calms the nervous system and signals that emotions are safe to express, even when change is still needed.

Emotional safety is also built through controlled reactions. Big reactions such as anger, sarcasm, withdrawal, or overcorrection, teach a spouse to brace themselves rather than open up. Calm, measured responses create predictability, and predictability builds trust. When a spouse knows what to expect emotionally, they are more willing to risk honesty. Safe relationships are not perfect, but they are emotionally consistent.

Conflict is the true test of emotional safety. Disagreements will happen, but how they are handled determines whether safety is strengthened or weakened. **Tone often matters more than content.** Staying focused on one is-

sue, allowing space for pauses, and refusing to
weaponize vulnerability are all ways to protect emotional safety during difficult conversations. When spouses fight with respect, conflict becomes a pathway to connection instead of division.

When emotional safety has been broken, rebuilding it takes time and intention. It requires acknowledging harm without defensiveness, taking responsibility without excuses, and demonstrating consistent change over time. Trust is not restored through words alone but through repeated actions that show safety is no longer at risk. Emotional safety returns slowly, one interaction at a time, as a spouse learns it is safe to trust again.

The fruit of emotional safety is profound. When judgment is removed, honesty increases. When fear is replaced with respect, conversations deepen. Emotional safety allows intimacy to grow because vulnerability no longer feels dangerous. In a judgment-free environment, love feels like rest rather than risk. Emotional safety does not eliminate truth; it creates a space where truth can be spoken, heard, and healed.

Emotional safety is not about walking on eggshells or avoiding hard conversations, it's about choosing love over the urge to be right. As we mentioned earlier, scripture reminds us in Ephesians 4:29 to *"speak in ways that build others up according to their needs,"* not according to our mood, tone, or need to win the moment. A judgment-free environment doesn't mean the truth gets watered down; it means the truth gets delivered with wisdom, grace, and timing. After all, even the best medicine can hurt if it's thrown instead of given. When safety exists, honesty no longer feels like a threat — it becomes a gift.

Most marital conflict doesn't start with a theological disagreement; it starts with tone, timing, or someone saying, "I'm fine" when they are clearly not. Proverbs 15:1 tells us that *"a gentle answer turns away wrath"*, which is biblical proof that volume has never saved a conversation. Emotional safety grows when we remember that our spouse is not the enemy and the goal is not victory, but unity. When we trade judgment for grace and sarcasm for curiosity, we don't just improve communication—we create a marriage where both people can breathe, speak, and be fully known without fear.

> **Emotional safety is not about walking on eggshells or avoiding hard conversations—it's about choosing love over the urge to be right**

How Small, Daily Affirmations Create Long-Term Intimacy

Most couples believe intimacy is built through big moments — anniversaries, getaways, candlelit dinners, and the occasional heartfelt speech that feels worthy of background music. Those moments matter, but Scripture, and real life, teach us something quieter and far more powerful: intimacy is built in the ordinary. The everyday words spoken while passing in the kitchen, the text sent during a busy workday, the comment made when no one else is listening. These are the bricks that build emotional closeness over time. As Jesus taught, faithfulness in small things leads to fruit in greater things (Luke 16:10). Marriage works the same way.

Daily affirmations create intimacy because they communicate one of the deepest human needs: *I see you.* Proverbs 16:24 reminds us that *"gracious words are a honeycomb, sweet to the soul and healing to the bones."* When a spouse hears consistent affirmation, it says, "Your effort matters. Your presence matters. You matter." Feeling seen produces emotional warmth, and emotional warmth opens the door to vulnerability. Intimacy grows where people feel noticed rather than overlooked. And yes, noticing counts even when the dishes aren't loaded "correctly."

Consistency is what transforms affirmation from encouragement into emotional safety. Random praise is nice — like finding five dollars in your pocket — but consistent affirmation builds security. When love is expressed daily, it reassures a spouse that affection isn't dependent on performance, moods, or perfection. Scripture tells us that *"perfect love drives out fear"* (1 John 4:18), and while no marriage offers perfect love, consistent affirmation drives out the fear of rejection, criticism, or emotional distance. Safety precedes closeness. You can't be fully known if you're constantly bracing for judgment.

Over time, affirmations do more than comfort — they shape identity. Words are powerful, especially when they are repeated. Proverbs 18:21 tells us that *"death and life are in the power of the tongue,"* and spouses wield that power daily, whether intentionally or not. When a husband consistently tells his wife she is capable, wise, and valued, those words take root. When a wife regularly affirms her husband's steadiness, integrity, or leadership, it reinforces who he believes he is. Eventually, people begin to live into the words spoken over them. Encouragement becomes formation.

Daily affirmation also counters what many couples don't see coming: negativity drift. Life is heavy. Work is stressful. Kids are loud. Laundry is endless. Without intention, marriages naturally slide toward criticism, silence, or emotional autopilot. Affirmation acts as an emotional deposit system, small, frequent investments that balance inevitable withdrawals. When conflict comes (and it will), a history of encouragement softens defenses and lowers walls. Ecclesiastes 4:12 reminds us that *"a cord of three strands is not quickly broken"*, and affirmation strengthens the strands that hold a marriage together.

Interestingly, the moments spouses remember most are rarely the grand gestures. They remember how it *felt* to be married. Did the relationship feel safe? Encouraging? Heavy? Joyful? Small affirmations shape the emotional memory of a marriage. Over time, couples associate one another with warmth rather than tension, appreciation rather than pressure. This emotional imprint quietly deepens intimacy. You don't need fireworks every night — just a steady glow.

Affirmation also plays a significant role in bridging emotional and physical intimacy. Emotional closeness fuels physical closeness. When a spouse feels emotionally pursued, appreciated, and desired, they are more open physically. Affirmation communicates desire in a relational, not transactional way. Song of Solomon is filled with verbal affirmation between spouses such as words of delight, admiration, and pursuit, reminding us that God designed spoken affection to stir both hearts and bodies. Turns out, "I appreciate you" is foreplay. Scripture knew this long before modern research caught up.

The beauty of daily affirmation is that it doesn't require eloquence or perfection — only intention. You don't need poetic skill or a theology degree. You need awareness. Missed days don't cancel progress; returning does. Lamentations 3:22–23 reminds us that *"God's mercies are new every morning"*, and marriage thrives when spouses adopt that same posture. Daily affirmation becomes less about emotion and more about obedience, choosing to speak life even when tired, distracted, or mildly annoyed.

At its core, **affirmation flows from gratitude**. Gratitude shifts focus from what is lacking to what is present. It softens entitlement and cultivates humility. Scripture urges believers to *"encourage one another daily"* (Hebrews 3:13), not occasionally, not when it's convenient, but daily. Gratitude expressed through affirmation reshapes how spouses see one another. Instead of keeping score, they begin to keep a record of appreciation.

Over the years, these small, daily affirmations create a culture within the marriage. Couples don't just remember what was said — they remember how it felt to live together. A marriage rich in encouragement leaves a legacy of warmth, respect, and connection. Intimacy becomes the natural byproduct of consistent kindness. Big moments still matter, but they stand on the foundation of small faithfulness.

In the end, intimacy isn't built in moments of perfection but in daily expressions of presence, appreciation, and affirmation. When love is spoken consistently, it is felt deeply. And over time, those small words become an unshakable bond one gracious sentence at a time.

Chapter Nine

The Power of Prayer and Spiritual Communication

Biblical Foundation: Matthew 18:19-20, 1 Thessalonians 5:17

Prayer is more than a personal spiritual discipline; it is a shared lifeline that binds hearts together before God. When a husband and wife pray together, they are not simply exchanging words, they are aligning their spirits, surrendering their marriage, and inviting heaven into the everyday moments of their lives. In a world that constantly pulls couples apart through busyness, distractions, and pressure, prayer becomes a sacred meeting place where unity is restored and strength is renewed.

There is a unique power that emerges when spouses seek God together. Scripture reminds us that *"where two or three gather in my name, there am I with them"* (Matthew 18:20). When a couple kneels side by side, they are declaring that their marriage is not sustained by effort alone, but by dependence on God. Prayer shifts the focus from "me versus you" to "us before Him," creating space for humility, grace, and mutual understanding to grow.

Praying together also deepens spiritual connection in ways conversation alone cannot. It softens hardened hearts, calms unspoken fears, and allows each spouse to hear not only God's voice, but one another's. In prayer, walls come down. Pride fades. Vulnerability rises. A spouse learns how the other truly thinks, hopes, struggles, and trusts God. Over time, this shared spiritual rhythm becomes an anchor that holds the marriage steady through storms and seasons of uncertainty.

This chapter explores the transformative power of prayer and spiritual connection when practiced together, not as a religious obligation, but as a relational gift. You will discover how prayer strengthens intimacy, encourages unity, and invites God to work in ways no human effort alone can accomplish. When a couple learns to seek God together, they don't just grow closer to Him, they grow closer to each other, building a marriage rooted in faith, resilience, and divine purpose.

How Praying Together Transforms Communication

Communication is one of the greatest gifts, and greatest challenges, in marriage. Words have the power to connect or divide, heal or wound, build trust or erode it. While many couples search for better techniques, tools, or strategies to improve communication, Scripture points us to a deeper starting place: the posture of the heart. One of the most transformative practices for marital communication is the simple, yet important, act of praying together. When a husband and wife pray together, communication is no longer driven by ego, emotion, or self-protection, but is re-centered on God, humility, and unity.

Praying together shifts the focus of communication away from winning an argument and toward surrendering to God's will. In prayer, pride is confronted and softened. It becomes difficult to cling to selfish agendas when both spouses acknowledge their dependence on God. Prayer reminds couples that their marriage does not exist for personal fulfillment alone, but for God's glory. When communication flows out of this understanding, conversations become less about control and more about cooperation. Instead of asking, *"How do I make my spouse see my point?"* the heart begins to ask, *"Lord, how do You want me to speak, and how do You want me to listen?"*

Another powerful effect of praying together is the way it softens hearts before words are ever exchanged. Many conflicts escalate not because of what is said, but because of the condition of the heart when it is said. Prayer has a unique ability to lower defenses, quiet emotional intensity, and create space for grace. It is difficult to pray sincerely with someone while holding onto bitterness toward them. In prayer, walls begin to come down, and compassion often replaces frustration. Hearts that are softened in God's presence are far more capable of hearing one another with patience and understanding.

Praying together also transforms the tone of communication within marriage. Couples who regularly pray together tend to speak more gently and respond more thoughtfully. Inviting the Holy Spirit into shared moments of prayer shapes not only spiritual intimacy but also verbal

expression. Prayer recalibrates the way spouses talk to each other, encouraging words that build rather than tear down. Over time, prayer influences everyday conversations, leading couples to choose language marked by kindness, restraint, and love. Communication becomes less reactive and more reflective of Christlike character.

One of the most damaging patterns in marriage communication is the mindset of "me versus you." Prayer dismantles this division by reminding couples that they are on the same side, kneeling before the same God. When spouses pray together, unity is reinforced. Problems are no longer framed as battles against each other, but challenges faced together under God's guidance. This shared spiritual posture makes it easier to admit fault, extend forgiveness, and pursue resolution rather than victory. Prayer redefines communication as a cooperative effort instead of a competitive exchange.

Praying together also invites a deeper level of honesty and vulnerability into the marriage. When spouses hear one another pray, they often gain insight into fears, struggles, hopes, and longings that may never surface in normal conversation. Prayer gives voice to the heart. It creates a sacred space where emotions can be expressed safely and sincerely before God. This vulnerability strengthens emotional intimacy and creates greater understanding between spouses, allowing communication to move beyond surface-level exchanges into a deeper connection.

Another way prayer transforms communication is by teaching couples to pause instead of reacting. In moments of tension, prayer introduces a holy pause that interrupts impulsive responses. Rather than allowing emotions to dictate words, couples learn to slow down and seek God's wisdom. This pause often prevents hurtful statements, misunderstandings, and unnecessary escalation. Over time, prayer trains couples to respond with discernment rather than react out of anger or fear, leading to healthier, more productive conversations.

As prayer becomes a consistent rhythm in marriage, its impact on communication grows long-term. Trust deepens, emotional safety increases, and difficult conversations become less intimidating. Couples who pray together regularly tend to resolve conflicts more quickly and approach challenges with humility. Prayer becomes not just a tool used in moments of crisis, but a foundation that shapes daily interaction. Communication rooted in prayer reflects a marriage continually shaped by God's grace.

Praying together does not require eloquence or perfection. It simply requires willingness. Whether prayer lasts thirty seconds or several minutes, the power lies not in the length of the prayer, but in the shared act of turning toward God together. As couples commit to praying with one another, they invite God into their communication, not merely to fix arguments, but to transform hearts. And when hearts are transformed, communication follows.

Inviting God into Daily Dialog

Inviting God into daily dialogue begins with reshaping how we understand communication with Him. For many believers, prayer has become a scheduled activity rather than a lived relationship. We talk to God in the morning, before meals, or at night, but rarely carry the conversation with us throughout the day. Yet Scripture paints a different picture, one of God walking with His people, not merely being summoned when needed. In Genesis, God walked with Adam in the garden, a symbol of relational closeness rather than ritual obligation. From the beginning, God desired a connection marked by openness, presence, and conversation. Daily dialogue with God is not about eloquence or length but about awareness and invitation.

Too often, we reserve prayer for moments of crisis while navigating ordinary life on our own. When tension rises, when fear sets in, or when decisions feel overwhelming, we suddenly remember to call on God. While God graciously meets us in those moments, He never intended to be a last resort. Scripture reminds us that *"in Him we live and move and have our being,"* meaning God is already present in every moment of our lives. Inviting Him into daily dialogue means welcoming Him into the mundane; our work, our conversations, our planning, and even our frustrations. It means acknowledging God not only when we are desperate for answers, but when we are simply living our everyday routines.

True dialogue with God also requires learning how to listen. Prayer is not meant to be a one-way exchange where we unload our thoughts and rush off to the next task. Listening creates space for God to shape our hearts, redirect our thinking, and calm our spirits. This listening rarely comes through audible words but through Scripture, inner conviction, a sense of peace or unease, or wisdom from trusted counsel. Stillness is often uncomfortable in a noisy, hurried world, yet it is in stillness that we become aware of God's presence. As we slow down, we learn to discern His voice from the many others competing for our attention.

Inviting God into daily dialogue also means allowing Him to shape our inner conversations. Much of life is interpreted through the silent dialogue in our minds such as what we tell ourselves about our circumstances, our worth, and our future. Left unchecked, these internal narratives can drift toward fear, pride, or self-reliance. God's Word calls us to renew our minds, replacing lies with truth and anxiety with trust. When God becomes part of our daily dialogue, our internal responses begin to align with His perspective rather than our emotions. We pause before reacting, seeking wisdom rather than assuming control.

As God reshapes our inner dialogue, it naturally affects how we speak to others. Words carry weight, especially in close relationships. Scripture reminds us that life and death are in the power of the tongue, and nowhere is this more evident than in marriage and family life. Inviting God into daily dialogue means asking Him to guide not only what we say but how and when we say it. It means praying before difficult conversations, seeking humility before correction, and choosing grace over defensiveness. When God influences our daily conversations with Him, our conversations with others become more thoughtful, patient, and life-giving.

Over time, daily dialogue with God becomes less about structured moments and more about continual awareness. This does not mean we abandon intentional prayer or Scripture reading, but that those disciplines fuel a deeper sense of God's nearness throughout the day. We begin to acknowledge Him in small decisions, quiet moments, and fleeting thoughts. Rather than striving to "pray more," we learn to include God more. Faith moves from being an isolated spiritual practice to a steady rhythm woven into everyday life.

Of course, obstacles often stand in the way of this kind of ongoing dialogue. **Busyness, distraction**, and **self-doubt** can make it difficult to remain spiritually attentive. Some believers struggle with feeling unworthy to approach God consistently, while others fear misinterpreting His guidance. Yet the relationship with God was never meant to be perfected through performance. God is patient, and spiritual growth is formed through consistency, not flawlessness. Every sincere invitation for God to be involved, no matter how small, deepens intimacy over time.

The fruit of inviting God into daily dialogue becomes evident in both subtle and significant ways. Peace replaces anxiety more quickly. Decisions are made with greater wisdom and humility. Relationships are marked by increased patience and understanding. Most importantly, faith matures from something we practice into someone we walk with. When God is welcomed into the small conversations of daily life, He transforms the larger ones. Daily dialogue does not just change how we pray, it changes how we live.

Listening to God's Voice Regarding Your Spouse

Marriage was never designed to be navigated by human wisdom alone. From the beginning, God intended marriage to be a sacred covenant that reflects His character, His love, and His faithfulness. When two people enter marriage, they don't simply join their lives together, they invite God into the center of their relationship. Because of this, learning to listen to God's voice regarding your spouse is not optional; it is essential. Without God's guidance, couples often react out of emotion, pride, or fear. With God's guidance, marriage becomes a place of growth, grace, and transformation.

Listening to God in marriage begins with understanding that His voice will never contradict His Word. God does not give personal direction that violates biblical truth.

Any thought, impression, or "leading" that results in control, manipulation, disrespect, or harm toward your spouse cannot be from Him. Scripture consistently calls spouses to love, honor, forgive, and serve one another. God's voice aligns with His revealed character; gentle, truthful, patient, and redemptive. When believers say, "God told me," it should always lead to Christlike behavior, not self-justification or spiritual dominance.

One of the greatest challenges in hearing God's voice regarding a spouse is learning to distinguish it from personal emotions. Hurt feelings can sound convincing. Anger can feel righteous. Fear can disguise itself as wisdom. But God's voice carries a different weight. It brings conviction without condemnation and clarity without chaos. While emotions often push us to react quickly, God's Spirit invites us to pause, reflect, and respond with wisdom. A helpful question in moments of tension is this: Is this leading me to love my spouse more deeply, or defend myself more aggressively? God's voice always draws us toward love.

Often, when we ask God to speak to us about our spouse, we expect Him to address what our spouse needs to change. Yet more often than not, God begins by speaking to us about ourselves. He searches our hearts, examines our motives, and gently exposes areas we need to work on. Instead of pointing fingers, God invites us to look inward. He may call us to listen more patiently, speak more gently, or release bitterness we've been holding onto. This inward work is not punishment; it is preparation. God is far more interested in shaping our hearts than fixing our spouse.

Conflict is one of the most revealing moments for discerning God's voice in marriage. When emotions are high, the flesh is loud, and wisdom can be drowned out. In these moments, listening to God often requires intentional stillness. God may prompt us to restrain when we want to lash out, to be humble when we want to be right, or to be silent when we want the final word. His voice in conflict rarely fuels escalation; instead, it brings calm, perspective, and a call to pursue peace. Couples who learn to pause and pray before reacting create space for God to redirect the conversation.

God's guidance in marriage is also deeply personal. While Scripture gives universal principles, the Holy Spirit applies them uniquely to each relationship. God knows your spouse fully — their wounds, fears, hopes, and needs — and He often calls us to love them in ways that don't come naturally. He may lead one spouse to offer affirmation rather than correction, patience rather than pressure, or presence rather than problem-solving. These promptings may challenge personal preferences, but obedience to God's voice produces lasting fruit.

There are also seasons when God seems silent regarding a spouse. Silence can feel unsettling, especially when answers are desired. Yet God's silence is never empty. Sometimes He is building trust, strengthening endurance, or teaching unconditional love. In these seasons, faithfulness becomes the lesson. God may be inviting obedience without explanation, choosing to love even when clarity is absent. Silence is not permission to act in the flesh; it is often an invitation to walk by faith.

Tuning our ears to God's voice in marriage requires intentional practice. Prayer, both personal and shared, keeps hearts aligned with God's perspective. Scripture renews the mind and anchors emotions in truth. Inviting God into daily moments, not just marital crises, creates ongoing sensitivity to His leading. Asking God questions rather than issuing demands creates humility and dependence. A simple prayer such as, "Lord, help me see my spouse the way You see them," can reshape attitudes and soften hearts.

When couples commit to listening to God together, the fruit becomes evident. Communication grows healthier. Conflict becomes less destructive, and trust deepens. Unity strengthens. Most importantly, marriage becomes a living testimony of Christ's love to a watching world. Listening to God's voice regarding your spouse transforms marriage from a battleground of opinions into a shared journey of obedience. In that space, love matures, grace multiplies, and God is glorified.

Speaking Scripture Over Your Marriage

Marriage is shaped not only by actions, but by words. What is consistently spoken within a relationship shapes its atmosphere, reinforces beliefs, and ultimately influences direction. From the opening pages of Scripture, we see that God Himself establishes reality through speech. "And God said..." is the repeated phrase of creation, reminding us that words carry creative power. In marriage, words can either cultivate life, hope, and unity, or sow division, discouragement, and distance. Speaking Scripture over your marriage is a deliberate choice to allow God's Word to define the relationship rather than emotions, circumstances, or past wounds.

The Bible makes it clear that words are never neutral. Proverbs tell us that death and life are in the power of the tongue, and those words do not lose their potency simply because they are spoken in the privacy of a home. In marriage, repeated phrases such as "you never," "you always," or "this will never change" slowly shape expectations and identity. Over time, they can harden hearts and narrow vision. In contrast, when God's Word is spoken aloud, declared in prayer, spoken in moments of tension, or whispered during seasons of weariness, it begins to reframe reality through truth rather than fear. Scripture interrupts destructive patterns by reminding a couple of what God says is possible.

Speaking Scripture over your marriage is not an act of denial, nor is it spiritual avoidance. It does not pretend that problems do not exist or that pain is imaginary. Rather, it is an act of faith that acknowledges reality while trusting God's greater truth. Faith, according to Scripture, calls things that are not as though they were, not because they are already visible, but because God is faithful to complete His work. When a couple speaks Scripture in the middle of conflict, exhaustion, or discouragement, they are choosing to agree with God's promises instead of allowing the moment to have the final word. This kind of faith does not ignore difficulty; it places difficulty under God's authority.

One of the most powerful effects of speaking Scripture is alignment. Marriage does not drift toward unity naturally; it must be continually realigned with God's design. Cultural expectations, personal history, and unmet desires constantly attempt to redefine what marriage should look like. Scripture pulls a couple back to God's original intent: **sacrificial love, mutual honor, humility**, and **oneness**. When a husband and wife regularly speak biblical truth over their relationship, they are reminded that marriage is not merely a contract between two people but a covenant before God. Scripture recenters the marriage on God's purpose rather than personal preference.

Over time, speaking Scripture helps establish a culture within the marriage and the home. Every home has a culture, whether it is intentionally shaped or not. Some homes are marked by tension and criticism, while others are characterized by peace and encouragement. Scripture spoken consistently instigates an environment where unity is valued and peace is protected. It invites God's presence into everyday moments and reinforces spiritual intimacy between spouses. When Scripture becomes part of a couple's shared language, it strengthens emotional safety and builds trust, even during disagreement.

There is also a spiritual dimension to marriage that cannot be ignored. Scripture teaches that marriage is a target of spiritual opposition, often attacked through lies, accusation, and division. Many marital conflicts escalate not because of the issue itself, but because unchallenged lies are allowed to take root — lies such as "this is hopeless," "you married the wrong person," or "change is impossible." The Word of God functions as both defense and weapon in these moments. Just as Jesus responded to temptation with Scripture, couples can resist discouragement and division by speaking God's truth aloud. Scripture exposes lies and restores perspective, reminding spouses that they are not enemies, but partners facing challenges together.

Wisdom is required, however, in how Scripture is spoken. There is a significant difference between **speaking Scripture over your spouse** and **speaking Scripture at your spouse**. God's Word is never meant to be weaponized in arguments or used to win debates. Quoting Scripture in frustration or pride often hardens hearts rather than softens them. Instead, Scripture should first be spoken in prayer, asking God to shape one's own heart before attempting to address a spouse. When Scripture flows from humility and love, it invites transformation rather than resistance. Spoken this way, it becomes a tool for healing, not just correction.

Consistency matters more than intensity when it comes to speaking Scripture over a marriage. This practice does not require long prayers or dramatic declarations. Simple, faithful habits over time produce lasting fruit. A couple may choose to speak one verse together each day, pray Scripture before difficult conversations, or declare God's promises during seasons of uncertainty. These small, intentional moments accumulate, reinforcing trust in God and in one another. Over time, Scripture becomes a steady rhythm rather than a last resort.

The impact of this practice often extends beyond the couple themselves. Children who grow up hearing Scripture spoken within their parents' marriage learn what faith looks like under pressure. They observe how God's Word shapes communication, conflict resolution, and forgiveness. Speaking Scripture in marriage becomes a form of discipleship, modeling reliance on God and demonstrating that faith is not reserved for church services but lived out in everyday relationships. The legacy of a Scripture-centered marriage often reaches far beyond what parents can immediately see.

There will be seasons when speaking Scripture feels difficult. Some moments are marked by deep pain, exhaustion, or emotional numbness, and in those times, even whispered prayers and short verses matter. God does not measure faith by volume or eloquence. He honors obedience and sincerity, even when strength feels limited. The Spirit helps when words feel hard to find, and Scripture spoken in weakness still carries power because it is God's Word, not human effort, that brings transformation.

Speaking Scripture over your marriage is an invitation for God to have the final word. When Scripture becomes the language of a marriage, truth replaces fear, hope confronts discouragement, and grace reshapes broken patterns. Circumstances may not change overnight, but hearts begin to soften, perspectives shift, and God's presence becomes more evident. A marriage anchored in God's Word learns to listen to His voice above all others, and that voice speaks life.

Using Prayer to Soften Hearts and Break Barriers

Prayer is one of the most powerful tools God has given His people, yet it is often misunderstood or misused. Many approach prayer as a way to change circumstances or persuade others to see things their way. However, biblical prayer works far deeper than surface-level outcomes. Prayer reaches into the heart, ours first, and then others, softening what has become hardened and breaking down barriers that human effort alone cannot overcome. In moments of relational strain, emotional distance, or unresolved conflict, prayer becomes the doorway through which God enters places we have been unable to reach.

At its core, **prayer is not about control but surrender**. When we come before God in prayer, we are inviting Him to do what we cannot do on our own. This is especially true when hearts are guarded, and communication feels impossible. In marriage, family relationships, and even within the church, prayer shifts the focus from fixing others to allowing God to refine us. David's prayer, *"Create in me a clean heart, O God, and renew a right spirit within me"* (Psalm 51:10), reminds us that transformation often begins internally. As God softens our hearts, defensiveness gives way to humility, and our posture toward others begins to change.

One of the greatest limitations in relational conflict is the belief that we can change another person through reasoning, pressure, or persistence. Scripture makes it clear that only God has the power to transform a heart truly. Proverbs 21:1 declares that *"the heart of a king is in the hand of the Lord, and He directs it as He pleases."* If God can turn the hearts of rulers, He can soften the hearts of spouses, children, and loved ones. Prayer acknowledges this truth and releases us from the burden of trying to control outcomes, trusting instead in God's ability to do what only He can.

Many barriers in relationships are not merely emotional but spiritual in nature. **Pride, fear, bitterness, offense**, and **unforgiveness** often take root beneath the surface, creating walls that conversations alone cannot tear down. The apostle Paul reminds us that the weapons we fight with are not of this world but have divine power to demolish strongholds (2 Corinthians 10:3–5). Prayer engages the spiritual realm, confronting unseen influences that shape attitudes and resistance. When prayer is applied consistently, strongholds begin to loosen, and emotional barriers start to crumble.

A significant shift occurs when we **stop praying against people** and **start praying for them**. Intercessory prayer reframes how we see the person on the other side of conflict. It becomes increasingly difficult to harbor resentment toward someone we regularly bring before God. Jesus instructed His followers to pray for those who wrong them, knowing that prayer would transform the heart of the one praying as much as the one being prayed for (Matthew 5:44). Job's restoration came only after he prayed for his friends, illustrating that prayer often unlocks healing in unexpected ways (Job 42:10).

Prayer also prepares the ground for healthy and productive conversations. While prayer does not replace communication, it prepares the soil so that words can be received rather than rejected. Scripture reminds us that there is a time for everything (Ecclesiastes 3:1), and prayer helps us discern the right moment and tone. When we pray before difficult discussions, we invite God to soften hearts, guard our words, and create an atmosphere of grace. Colossians 4:6 urges believers to let their speech be full of grace, and prayer is often what makes that possible.

How we pray matters as much as what we pray. Prayer fueled by frustration seeks immediate change, while prayer rooted in faith trusts God's timing and process. James warns believers not to pray with doubt or a divided heart (James 1:6–8). Faith-filled prayer rests in God's character rather than visible outcomes. Hebrews 11:6 reminds us that faith pleases God, and trusting Him, even when nothing appears to be changing, strengthens our spiritual endurance.

Heart transformation is often a process rather than a single moment. Jesus encouraged persistence in prayer, teaching that we should not lose heart when answers seem delayed (Luke 18:1). God works progressively, shaping hearts layer by layer. Delay does not mean denial; it often means God is doing deeper work than we can see. Galatians 6:9 encourages believers not to grow weary, reminding us that perseverance will eventually yield fruit.

Prayer and forgiveness are deeply connected. Unforgiveness hardens hearts and blocks spiritual growth, while forgiveness opens the door for healing. Jesus taught that forgiveness should accompany prayer, instructing His followers to forgive as they pray (Mark 11:25). Forgiveness does not minimize pain or dismiss wrongdoing, but it releases the grip of bitterness. Ephesians 4:31–32 calls believers to let go of resentment and extend grace, reflecting the forgiveness we have received through Christ.

In the end, prayer teaches us to trust God with outcomes we cannot control. Our responsibility is obedience; transformation belongs to God. Proverbs 3:5–6 reminds us to *"trust the Lord with all our hearts and not lean on our own understanding."* Prayer anchors us in peace even before circumstances change. God promises that His word *"will not return empty but will accomplish what He intends"* (Isaiah 55:11). When we commit to prayer, we can rest in the assurance that softened hearts and broken barriers are never beyond God's reach.

Michelle and I both know that if prayer had not become the foundation of our communication, our marriage would not look anything like it does today. Early on, we inflicted real damage on each other, not because we didn't love one another, but because we didn't yet know how to communicate without wounding. Words were used as weapons, silence became punishment, and pride often spoke louder than grace. Conversations quickly turned into battlegrounds where the goal was to win, not to understand. Left to ourselves, we would have continued repeating the same cycles, reopening the same wounds, and drifting further apart with every unresolved conflict.

Prayer changed everything, not overnight, but decisively. When we began praying before hard conversations, during moments of tension, and even after words had already been spoken, God started softening hearts that had grown guarded. Prayer slowed us down, humbled us, and invited God into the space between our words and our reactions.

It didn't erase the past, but it redeemed it. What once would have ended in defensiveness began to open the door to listening, repentance, and healing. Our story stands as living proof that no amount of damage is beyond God's ability to restore. If prayer can rebuild what was broken between us, then there is always hope, no matter how far gone a marriage or relationship may seem.

Rebuilding Trust Through Better Conversations

Proverbs 10:9, Psalm 51:6

Trust is the quiet backbone of every healthy marriage, it doesn't make a lot of noise, but when it's missing, everyone feels it. You can have great chemistry, shared values, and even solid communication tools, but without trust, conversations turn into courtroom cross-examinations and simple questions start sounding like accusations. "Where were you?" isn't just small talk when trust is shaky — it's a full investigation. Trust creates safety, and safety is what allows honesty, vulnerability, and real connection to flourish between spouses.

In many ways, trust is the litmus test of a marriage's strength and resilience. When trust is strong, hard conversations don't break the relationship — they build it. Disagreements become discussions, not disasters. Missteps are met with grace rather than suspicion, and apologies are received rather than analyzed for hidden motives. Trust doesn't mean perfection; it means believing your spouse is for you, even when communication gets messy. A marriage anchored in trust can bend without breaking, laugh in the middle of tension, and keep moving forward because both hearts know they're safe in the conversation, even when the words are hard.

So, let's start learning how to rebuild and strengthen trust the right way by having better conversations that replace defensiveness with understanding, fear with safety, and distance with connection.

The Connection Between Honesty, Transparency, and Trust

Trust in marriage does not appear out of thin air, it is built through a steady relationship between honesty and transparency. While these words are often used interchangeably, they are not the same thing and confusing them can quietly undermine even well-intentioned relationships. Honesty is telling the truth when asked. Transparency is willingly offering the truth before suspicion ever needs to knock. Trust is what grows when both become a consistent pattern rather than a special occasion.

Honesty is the foundation of trust. Without it, trust cannot survive. When a spouse begins to question whether the truth will be told, every conversation becomes unstable. Even small lies or half-truths create uncertainty, and uncertainty breeds distance. Many couples don't lose trust because of one major betrayal, but because of repeated moments where clarity was replaced with confusion. When honesty becomes selective, trust becomes fragile.

Transparency, however, is what strengthens and sustains trust over time. Transparency goes beyond answering questions accurately — it invites your spouse into your thoughts, intentions, struggles, and decisions. It says, *"You don't have to guess what's happening inside me."* In marriage, transparency removes the burden of assumption. When information is withheld, the human mind fills in the gaps, and it rarely fills them with grace. Transparency eliminates unnecessary fear and allows emotional intimacy to grow.

One of the most overlooked threats to trust is secrecy that falls short of outright lying. A spouse can technically tell the truth while still hiding important pieces of their inner world. Omission often feels safer than deception, but it carries a similar cost. Hidden emotions, private resentments, undisclosed spending, or unspoken temptations slowly erode trust. Secrecy sends an unspoken message: *"There are parts of me you are not safe to know."* Over time, that message damages the connection more deeply than many couples realize.

Transparency feels risky because it requires vulnerability. It exposes fears, weaknesses, and areas of failure that we would rather keep protected. Many spouses avoid transparency not because they want to deceive, but because they fear conflict, rejection, or misunderstanding. Yet avoiding transparency in the name of self-protection almost always produces the opposite result. What feels like safety in the moment often turns into emotional distance over time. In marriage, closeness is built through shared truth, not managed impressions.

Trust is not built through dramatic gestures or emotional speeches; it is formed in consistent, everyday conversations. Small moments matter more than grand promises. Trust grows when words match actions, when mistakes are admitted quickly, and when follow-through becomes predictable. Each honest conversation reinforces the belief that "I can rely on you." Over time, consistency turns honesty and transparency into credibility, and credibility creates security.

Healthy communication strengthens the relationship between honesty, transparency, and trust. When conversations are safe, honesty becomes easier. When honesty is welcomed, transparency increases. When transparency becomes normal, trust deepens. This creates a reinforcing cycle that strengthens the marriage from the inside out. Couples who communicate well don't avoid hard conversations; they navigate them with confidence because trust provides a safety net beneath the words.

Grace plays a critical role in sustaining this cycle. Trust cannot grow in an environment where honesty is punished or vulnerability is met with shame. If transparency consistently leads to anger, defensiveness, or control, secrecy will eventually replace openness. Grace does not ignore wrongdoing, but it creates space for truth to be shared without fear of destruction. In marriages where grace is practiced, honesty feels safer, and restoration becomes possible.

When trust has been damaged, rebuilding it requires intentional effort. Honesty must become uncompromising, transparency must become proactive, and consistency must replace excuses. Trust is restored not by demanding it, but by demonstrating reliability over time. Words may reopen the door, but actions keep it open. As safety returns, trust begins to rebuild, not immediately, but steadily and securely.

At its core, trust is not built by knowing everything about your spouse; it is built by knowing they are willing to share anything with you. When honesty and transparency become habits rather than strategies, trust stops being fragile and starts becoming resilient. And from that place of trust, conversations no longer feel like battles to survive, but bridges that strengthen the marriage with every step forward.

How to Restore Communication After Betrayal or Broken Promises

Restoring communication after betrayal or broken promises is one of the hardest, and most sacred journeys a marriage can take. Betrayal doesn't just wound the heart; it fractures the very language a couple uses to connect. Words feel unsafe, silence feels protective, and even well-intended conversations can feel like walking through emotional landmines. When trust is broken, communication doesn't simply pause, it changes. And pretending otherwise only deepens the damage.

One of the most important steps in restoring communication is acknowledging the reality of the wound. Betrayal must be named before healing can begin. Whether the betrayal was a major breach or a series of broken promises, minimizing the pain does not speed up recovery, it delays it. Hurt that goes unacknowledged doesn't disappear; it just goes underground, where it resurfaces later as resentment, distance, or emotional shutdown. Honest acknowledgment says, "What happened mattered, and so do your feelings about it."

When trust is broken, communication often breaks down because fear takes over. The betrayed spouse fears being hurt again. The betraying spouse fears constant reminders of failure. Defensiveness replaces curiosity, silence replaces vulnerability, and anger often becomes the loudest voice in the room. This breakdown is not a sign of weakness; it is a natural response to emotional injury. Understanding this helps couples stop attacking each other for struggling and start addressing the real issue — the loss of safety.

Michelle and I know this firsthand. There was a season in our marriage where we both betrayed each other's trust in different ways. No dramatic movie-scene betrayals, but real ones nonetheless — broken promises, unmet expectations, unspoken resentments, and moments where honesty and transparency took a back seat to self-protection. We didn't just wake up one day with poor communication; we earned it. And rebuilding it required humility, patience, and more awkward conversations than either of us would like to admit. Rebuilding trust includes realizing you're not always the hero in your own story.

For the spouse who broke trust, restoring communication begins with full owner-ship without defensiveness. True accountability doesn't rush to explanations or soften responsibility with "but." Saying "I was wrong" without conditions is one of the most powerful ways to reopen communication. Ownership validates the injured spouse's pain and begins restoring emotional safety. Partial ownership, on the other hand, sounds like honesty but feels like avoidance, and it keeps walls firmly in place.

Before meaningful communication can be restored, emotional safety must be re-es-tablished. Deep conversations cannot thrive in an environment where one spouse feels pressured to forgive quickly or "just move on." **Safety is rebuilt through consistent behavior, patience, and respect for the healing process.** In our marriage, Michelle and I had to learn that timing mattered. Not every conversation needed to happen immediately, and not every question needed a perfectly worded answer. Sometimes safety meant slowing down rather than pushing forward.

After betrayal, honesty must become uncompromising, and transparency must be-come proactive. This is not about living under surveillance or earning forgiveness through information overload. It is about restoring credibility. Trickle truth and selective disclo-sure keep wounds open. Proactive transparency says, *"I'm not waiting for suspicion to ask — I'm choosing openness because trust matters."* Over time, this consistency rebuilds confidence in the relationship.

Listening also takes on a new role after betrayal. Restored communication requires listening without defending, correcting, or fixing. The injured spouse often needs to say the same thing more than once, not because they enjoy reliving pain, but because healing is rarely linear. Michelle and I learned that repetition was part of recovery. If you're thinking, "Didn't we already talk about this?", congratulations, you're probably still healing. Listening well in those moments communicates safety far louder than words ever could.

Triggers and emotional flooding are another reality couples must learn to navigate. Certain words, situations, or tones can instantly reignite old pain. Healthy communication includes recognizing triggers, calling time-outs without abandoning the conversation, and agreeing on boundaries around tone and timing. Stepping away is not quitting, it's protecting progress. In our experience, some of our best conversations happened after we learned when to pause.

Ultimately, **communication is restored not by words alone, but by consistent action**. Apologies may reopen the door, but reliability keeps it open. Keeping small promises, showing up emotionally, and remaining predictable rebuild trust brick by brick. Michelle and I didn't rebuild trust with one emotional conversation, we rebuilt it through hundreds of ordinary moments where words and actions finally matched again.

Time is an unavoidable part of healing, but time alone does not heal wounds — intentional effort does. There will be setbacks, emotional flare-ups, and moments where it feels like progress has vanished. These moments are not proof of failure; they are part of the process. Grace allows room for healing, while accountability ensures growth. Both are necessary for communication to recover truly.

When restoration feels overwhelming, outside help can be a gift. Counseling or pastoral guidance provides structure, safety, and perspective during seasons where emotions cloud clarity. Seeking help is not a sign that a marriage is failing, it is often evidence that it matters deeply.

Betrayal may silence a marriage for a season, but it need not define its future. When couples commit to rebuilding communication with honesty, transparency, grace, and consistency, trust can return, often stronger than before. Michelle and I are living proof that broken trust does not have to mean broken marriage. With intentional communication, what was once fractured can become fortified, and conversations that once felt dangerous can become the very place healing takes root.

> **Time is an unavoidable part of healing, but time alone does not heal wounds—intentional effort does**

Consistency: Proving Change Through Words and Actions

Consistency is where change stops being something you *say* and starts becoming something your spouse can actually trust. In marriage, real change is not proven by emotional speeches, good intentions, or even sincere apologies — patterns over time prove it. Anyone can promise to do better in the heat of a hard conversation. Consistency is what answers the quiet question every wounded spouse is asking: *Is this going to last, or is this just another phase?*

One of the biggest misunderstandings couples have about change is confusing intention with transformation. Most spouses genuinely *intend* to change, but intention alone does not rebuild trust. Patterns do. A pattern of honesty, follow-through, and emotional steadiness communicates far more than words ever could. Michelle and I learned this the hard way. There were seasons when we both meant well, apologized sincerely, and then slowly slipped back into old habits. Good intentions felt comforting in the moment, but they didn't restore trust. Only new, repeated behaviors did.

Words matter, but words without action eventually become noise. Repeated promises without follow-through don't just disappoint, they actually deepen distrust. After a while, even heartfelt apologies can sound hollow if behavior remains unchanged. In our marriage, we had to accept a humbling truth: the more we talked about changing, the less believable it became. Ironically, trust began to return when we talked less and lived more. Consistent action preached louder sermons than our best explanations ever could.

Trust is rebuilt in small, often unimpressive moments, or drops. It grows when commitments are kept, when tone stays respectful under stress, and when honesty shows up even when it's uncomfortable. Big gestures are memorable, but small daily faithfulness is transformative. Michelle and I didn't rebuild trust with grand romantic resets, we rebuilt it by doing what we said we would do, especially when no one was applauding. (Turns out, consistency is far less glamorous than apologies, but far more effective.)

Time plays a critical role in bringing about change, but time alone is never enough. Time without effort allows wounds to harden. Change must be consistent *over* time to become credible. Trust doesn't return because enough days have passed; it returns because enough evidence has been provided. Michelle and I learned patience on both sides, one of us learning to stay steady in growth, the other learning to observe patterns without rushing the outcome.

Consistency is most clearly tested when old wounds are triggered. Anyone can behave well when things are calm; growth is revealed when stress shows up. How a spouse responds in those moments either reinforces healing or reopens wounds. In our marriage, some of the greatest

trust-building moments came when old issues resurfaced, and we responded differently than before. Not perfectly, but differently. Calm replaced defensiveness. Listening replaced explaining. Those moments mattered deeply.

Setbacks are inevitable, but they don't erase progress unless they're mishandled. Consistency does not require perfection — it requires ownership. When failure is met with humility instead of excuses, trust continues to grow. Michelle and I had to learn that repairing quickly mattered more than pretending we never failed. Saying, "I messed up, and I'm committed to doing better," became a powerful consistency marker in our relationship.

Accountability also plays a key role in sustaining change. Consistency is difficult in isolation. Outside support, clear boundaries, and agreed-upon expectations provide structure that protects progress. In our journey, accountability helped ensure that growth wasn't self-declared but observable. It wasn't about control; it was about support.

As consistency took root, emotional safety began to return. Predictable behavior reduced anxiety. Reliability restored openness. Communication improved not because we tried harder to talk, but because trust made conversation feel safe again. Consistency didn't just rebuild trust; it reshaped how we communicated.

Recognizing change without rushing trust requires patience from both spouses. The one changing must remain steady without demanding immediate affirmation. The one healing must observe honestly without moving the goalposts. Trust returns when consistency becomes normal, not performative.

In the end, consistency is what makes apologies believable and change safe. Michelle and I learned that real transformation happens quietly, through repeated choices made long after the emotional conversations end. When words and actions align over time, trust no longer has to be forced. It simply returns, one faithful drop at a time.

Creating New Communication Habits that Strengthen Trust

Creating new communication habits that strengthen trust is not about becoming better arguers, it's about becoming safer partners. After trust has been damaged and consistency has begun to take root, couples often assume they can return to "normal." But normal is usually what got them into trouble in the first place. Old communication patterns were formed under old levels of trust, stress, and immaturity. New trust requires new rhythms. Healing doesn't come from repeating the past more carefully; it comes from intentionally building something different.

One of the first lessons Michelle and I had to learn was that trust grows in predictable environments. When communication feels unpredictable, tone changes suddenly, conversations explode without warning, or silence replaces engagement and trust stays fragile. Predictable communication doesn't mean boring conversations; it means emotional safety. Knowing when conversations will take place, how concerns will be raised, and how conflict will be handled reduces anxiety and builds confidence. In our marriage, simply agreeing *on when we would talk about hard things reduced tension more* than we expected. (Turns out surprise emotional ambushes are rarely received as acts of love.)

Healthy communication habits also require **making honesty the default, not the emergency response**. Many couples only become honest when something is already wrong. By then, emotions are high, and trust is already under strain. Michelle and I learned that small, honest check-ins, sharing frustrations early, expressing needs clearly, and naming concerns before they grew, prevented far bigger conflicts later. Honest conversations became less dramatic and more routine, making trust feel normal rather than fragile.

Another trust-strengthening habit is **learning to speak without defensiveness**. Defensiveness doesn't protect a marriage — it protects pride. When every conversation turns into self-justification, trust slowly erodes. We had to learn that owning impact mattered more than explaining intent. Saying, "I see how that hurt you," built far more trust than saying, "That's not what I meant." Curiosity opened doors that defensiveness slammed shut.

Listening also had to change. Trust deepens when spouses listen to understand rather than to win. Reflecting what was heard, asking clarifying questions, and slowing conversations down all signal safety. Michelle and I discovered that many of our conflicts weren't about disagreement, they were about misunderstanding. Feeling understood often mattered more than being agreed with. And yes, sometimes listening meant resisting the urge to interrupt with a solution before the sentence was finished. Growth is humbling like that.

Creating regular rhythms for communication is another habit that strengthens trust. When conversations only happen during conflict, communication becomes associated with stress. Scheduled check-ins, weekly conversations, daily emotional temperature checks, or brief follow-ups after disagreements, normalize communication. In our marriage, this turned conversations from something we braced for into something we expected. Trust grows when communication is proactive instead of reactive.

Avoidance is another old habit that must be replaced. Silence may feel peaceful, but unresolved issues don't disappear — they accumulate. Healthy engagement teaches couples how to stay connected even when things are uncomfortable. Michelle and I had to learn that disagreements

didn't threaten our marriage, avoiding them did. Learning how to stay present without escalating became a cornerstone of rebuilding trust.

Repair language also became a habit rather than a last resort. Apologizing quickly, naming misunderstandings early, and using phrases like "Help me understand" kept small issues from becoming trust fractures. Repair doesn't mean admitting fault for everything, it means prioritizing connection over ego. Trust grows when repair is normal, not dramatic.

Affirmation and appreciation further reinforce trust. Noticing effort, acknowledging growth, and expressing gratitude remind a spouse that progress is seen and valued. Michelle and I learned that celebrating improvement, even imperfect improvement, encouraged consistency. Trust grows when spouses feel recognized, not scrutinized.

Of course, communication habits fail if the actions they support don't. Words and behavior must align. Following through, keeping commitments, and remaining emotionally available reinforce credibility. Over time, communication feels safe again because it's supported by consistent action.

New habits take time to feel natural. At first, they feel awkward, forced, and occasionally clumsy. But habits don't need to feel natural to be effective, they need to be consistent. Michelle and I had plenty of moments where new communication skills felt scripted or uncomfortable, but consistency eventually turned effort into instinct.

In the end, trust is strengthened not by avoiding hard conversations, but by learning how to have them well. Creating new communication habits transforms conversations from places of fear into places of connection. When honesty is routine, listening is intentional, repair is quick, and engagement is steady, trust stops being something you worry about losing, and starts becoming the environment your marriage lives in every day.

Guarding Your Words from Manipulation or Passive Aggression

Guarding your words from manipulation or passive aggression is one of the most important, and humbling, communication shifts a marriage can make. Words are meant to connect, clarify, and heal, yet when fear, resentment, or unmet needs creep in, those same words can quietly turn into weapons. Manipulation and passive aggression rarely sound harsh on the surface; they often sound reasonable, spiritual, or even polite. But beneath them is a lack of honesty that slowly erodes trust and emotional safety.

Michelle and I had to learn that unhealthy communication patterns usually don't come from a desire to harm, they come from a desire to protect ourselves. When direct honesty felt risky, indirect communication felt safer. Manipulation whispered, *If I say this just right, I'll get what I need without conflict.* Passive aggression said, *I'll express my frustration without actually having to talk about it.* Neither brought peace. Both created confusion. (And just for the record, sarcasm is not a "communication style" — it's just anger wearing a funny hat!)

Manipulation in marriage often shows up subtly. It can look like guilt-based language, selective silence, spiritual pressure, or playing the victim to avoid responsibility.

Passive aggression tends to surface as sarcasm, withdrawal, backhanded compliments, or the infamous phrase, "I'm fine," when everyone in the room knows that is absolutely not true. These patterns force a spouse to guess what's really happening, and trust cannot grow where clarity is missing.

The reason these habits damage trust so deeply is that they remove emotional safety. Manipulation makes a spouse feel managed instead of respected. Passive aggression makes a spouse feel punished rather than invited to be honest. Over time, conversations become exhausting because nothing is said plainly. Michelle and I discovered that indirect communication didn't reduce conflict, it multiplied it. We weren't avoiding hard conversations; we were delaying them and adding frustration along the way.

At the root of manipulative or passive-aggressive speech is often fear—fear of conflict, rejection, not being heard, or losing control. Recognizing this helped us move from blame to responsibility. Instead of asking, *"Why are you talking to me like that?"* we began asking ourselves, *"Why am I afraid to say this directly?"* That shift was uncomfortable, but freeing.

Avoiding the Manipulation Roadmap

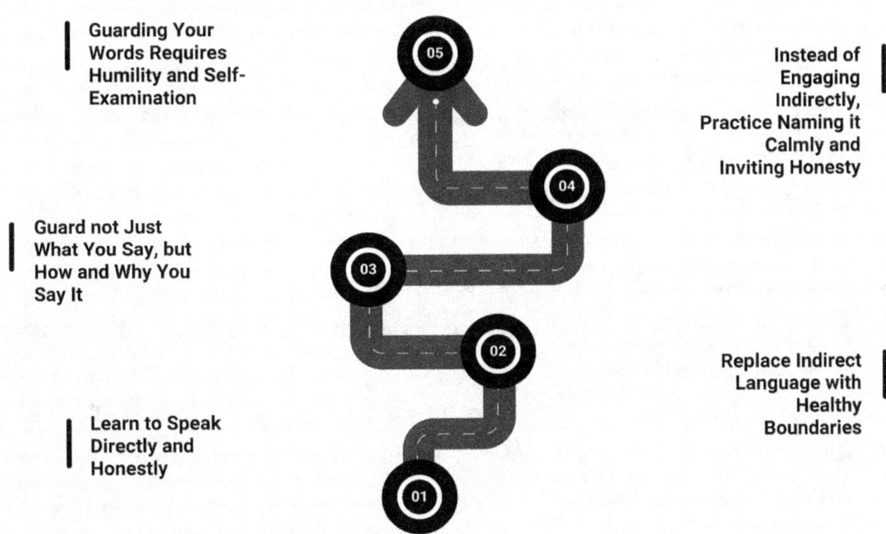

Learning to speak directly and honestly became a turning point for us. Direct communication doesn't accuse or demand; it names needs, feelings, and concerns clearly. Saying, "That hurt me," built far more trust than sarcasm ever did. Asking plainly for what we needed felt vulnerable at first, but it removed the emotional fog that manipulation creates. Honesty stopped being a confrontation and started becoming an invitation.

Replacing indirect language with healthy boundaries was another major step. Instead of withdrawing, we learned to say, "I need a little time to cool down, but I want to come back and talk." Instead of hinting, we learned to ask. Boundaries brought clarity without hostility. They allowed us to stay honest without being harsh and to stay connected without being controlling.

We also had to learn to guard not just *what* we said, but *how* and *why* we said it. Tone matters. Timing matters. Motive matters. A true test became asking, "Am I trying to build a connection or get leverage?" That question alone saved us from countless unnecessary arguments. Words spoken to clarify build trust; words spoken to control destroy it.

Equally important was learning how to respond when manipulation or passive aggression showed up. Instead of engaging indirectly, we practiced naming it calmly and inviting honesty. Saying, "Help me understand what you're really feeling," kept conversations grounded. Clarity became our antidote. We learned that refusing to play guessing games wasn't unloving, it was healthy.

Guarding your words also requires humility and self-examination. Growth happens when spouses are willing to admit, "I said that to get a reaction," or "I avoided being honest because I was afraid." Michelle and I both had to repent of control-based communication and choose truth over comfort. Spiritual maturity doesn't eliminate conflict; it cleans up how we speak in the middle of it.

The good news is that manipulative and passive-aggressive habits can be unlearned. As words become cleaner and clearer, trust grows stronger. Conversations become safer. Needs are expressed openly. Resentment loses its hiding places. When communication is direct, respectful, and honest, marriage becomes less about managing tension and more about building connection.

Healthy words don't pressure, punish, or provoke, they invite, clarify, and build. When Michelle and I learned to guard our words, we didn't just improve communication, we restored trust. And while we're still learning, one thing is certain: honesty may feel risky in the moment, but it is always safer than manipulation in the long run.

Hopefully, within this chapter, we have conveyed in an understandable way how rebuilding trust through better conversations is not about saying all the right things, it's about creating an environment where honesty, safety, and consistency can take root. Trust is restored when words are clear, motives are clean, and actions follow through over time.

As couples learn to communicate without defensiveness, manipulation, or avoidance, conversations stop feeling like threats and start becoming bridges. Better conversations don't erase the past, but they do reshape the future by proving that growth is real, change is lasting, and connection is still possible.

Ultimately, **trust returns when communication becomes a place of refuge instead of fear**. When spouses commit to speaking truth with grace, listening with humility, and repairing quickly when missteps happen, trust is no longer something that has to be demanded or defended — it is quietly rebuilt. Rebuilding trust is rarely fast and never perfect, but it is always worth the effort. When conversations are handled with intention and care, marriage becomes resilient again, and what was once broken can become stronger than it was before.

Chapter Eleven

Creating a Communication Rhythm for Your Marriage

Biblical Foundation: Ecclesiastes 3:1-7, Amos 3:3

Marriage does not usually fall apart because of one explosive argument, it erodes slowly through missed moments, unspoken expectations, and conversations that never quite happen. Most couples talk every day, yet still feel unheard, misunderstood, or emotionally disconnected. The issue is rarely a lack of words; it's a lack of rhythm. Without a healthy pattern for communication, even well-intentioned conversations can feel chaotic, reactive, or exhausting rather than life-giving.

God is a God of rhythm and order. From the cadence of creation to the steady faithfulness of His promises, Scripture reveals a divine design where consistency brings stability and growth. In the same way, communication in marriage was never meant to be sporadic or crisis driven. When couples only talk deeply when something is wrong, communication becomes associated with tension instead of connection. A communication rhythm reframes conversation as a regular, intentional practice — one that builds trust, safety, and unity over time.

A healthy communication rhythm doesn't mean scripted conversations or forced checklists. It means creating predictable spaces where both spouses know they will be heard, valued, and engaged. It allows difficult topics to surface gently, before they harden into resentment. It makes room for joy, affirmation, prayer, and alignment so that emotional intimacy grows alongside spiritual intimacy. When communication becomes rhythmic, marriage begins to feel less like emotional whiplash and more like a shared journey.

In this chapter, we will explore how to establish a communication rhythm that fits your marriage, your season of life, and your unique personalities. You'll learn how intentional timing, shared expectations, and biblical principles can transform the way you talk, and just as importantly, the way you listen. Communication is not simply about solving problems; it is about stewarding the sacred connection God entrusted to you. When your conversations move in step with grace, truth, and consistency, your marriage gains a steady heartbeat — one that sustains love for the long run.

Establishing Daily, Weekly, and Monthly "Connection Points"

Most marriages don't struggle because couples refuse to talk, they struggle because couples only talk when something is wrong. Communication becomes reactive instead of relational, and conversations feel like emergency meetings rather than moments of connection. If you're honest, many of your "deep talks" probably begin with phrases like *"We need to talk"* or *"Can I say something without you getting mad?"* That's not a rhythm; that's a fire drill.

God designed marriage to thrive on intentional connection, not emotional last-minute scrambles. Scripture reminds us that *"Let all things be done decently and in order"* (1 Corinthians 14:40). That principle doesn't just apply to church services; it applies to relationships. When communication has no rhythm, emotions pile up, assumptions grow, and distance sneaks in quietly. But when couples establish regular connection points — daily, weekly, and monthly — communication becomes a source of safety instead of stress.

REGULAR CONNECTION POINTS

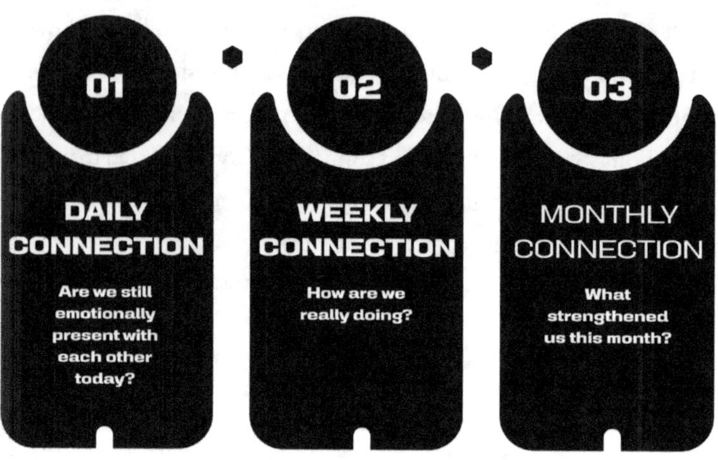

Daily connection points are the smallest but most powerful conversations in a marriage. These are not long, dramatic heart-to-hearts; they are simple, intentional moments of presence. A few focused minutes at the end of the day can do more for intimacy than an entire weekend getaway spent distracted. Daily connection answers one essential question: *"Are we still emotionally present with each other today?"* Scripture says, *"Be quick to hear, slow to speak, slow to anger"* (James 1:19), yet many couples rush past listening because life feels loud and urgent. Daily check-ins slow things down. They create space to ask, "What was heavy today?" or *"Where did you feel God show up?"* Sometimes, the most spiritual thing you can do for your marriage is put your phone down and actually look at your spouse.

These daily moments also guard against emotional drift. When couples skip daily connection, they don't usually notice it at first. They still share a house, a bed, and a calendar — but not a heart. Over time, marriage begins to feel more like roommates coordinating schedules than partners sharing life. A brief prayer together, even one that feels awkward or unfinished, can realign hearts. Ecclesiastes 4:12 reminds us that *"a cord of three strands is not quickly broken."* Daily prayer, however short, weaves God into the ordinary moments where intimacy is quietly built.

Weekly connection points provide space for alignment and repair. While daily conversations maintain closeness, weekly conversations help couples zoom out and ask, *"How are we really doing?"* This is where issues that don't fit into quick check-ins finally get air. Weekly connection works best when it's predictable, a set time that both spouses can count on. Predictability builds emotional safety. When your spouse knows there will be space to talk, they don't have to store frustration all week like leftovers that eventually go bad.

Weekly conversations allow couples to address tension before it turns into resentment. Scripture encourages us, *"Do not let the sun go down on your anger"* (Ephesians 4:26), not because conflict is sinful, but because unresolved conflict is corrosive. Weekly rhythms also create room for celebration. Too many couples only review what went wrong, forgetting to acknowledge growth, answered prayers, and moments of grace. Gratitude softens hearts. Proverbs 17:22 tells us that *"a joyful heart is good medicine"*, and sometimes laughter during a weekly check-in is exactly what a tired marriage needs. Yes, you can talk about serious things and still smile!

Monthly connection points take communication beyond maintenance and into mission. These conversations are less about the week-to-week grind and more about who you are becoming together. Monthly rhythms invite reflection: What strengthened us this month? Where did we struggle? What is God inviting us into next? Without these conversations, marriages can unknowingly drift from God's original design, pulled instead by busyness, pressure, or survival mode.

Monthly connection points are also the right space for deeper conversations about values, goals, finances, intimacy, and spiritual growth. These are not conversations to squeeze in between errands. They require margin and intentionality. Amos 3:3 asks, *"Can two walk together unless they are agreed?"* Agreement doesn't happen accidentally; it happens when couples slow down long enough to listen, pray, and recalibrate. Monthly conversations help ensure that marriage stays aligned with God's purpose rather than merely functioning efficiently.

The goal of daily, weekly, and monthly connection points is not perfection, it's faithfulness. Some weeks you'll miss your rhythm. Some days, the conversation will be clumsy. That's okay. Rhythm is about returning, not performing. Lamentations 3:22–23 reminds us that *"God's mercies are new every morning"*, and the same grace applies to marriage. Small, consistent moments of connection, repeated over time, build trust, intimacy, and resilience.

Marriage flourishes when communication becomes a habit, not a reaction. When couples create intentional rhythms, they stop asking, *"Why do we only talk when things are bad?"* and start experiencing conversations that heal, strengthen, and unite. In a world that constantly pulls spouses in different directions, these connection points anchor marriage to what matters most — love, unity, and a shared walk with God.

The Importance of Check-Ins and Emotional Updates

Whenever someone tells me marriage is easier than dating, I immediately wonder what universe they're living in — Disneyland? Communication in marriage is both simple and incredibly complex: simple because we all know what it feels like to be heard, and complex because daily life, stress, and old habits can drag even the best intentions into silence. In our hurried world, many couples talk for less than 3 minutes a day — yes, that's less than 20 minutes per week, according to popular estimates — which often leaves them feeling more like roommates than life partners.

Check-ins and emotional updates are not just "nice ideas"; they are the **lifeblood of relational connection**. At their core, check-ins are the practice of pausing to ask one another about the inner world of the heart, not just the schedule, laundry list, or what's for dinner, but *how are you really doing?* If communication is the bloodstream of marriage, then check-ins are the heartbeats that keep that blood flowing healthily. Paul's wisdom to the early church is fitting here: *"Let each of you look not only to his own interests, but also to the interests of others"* (Philippians 2:4). In marriage, this means looking *into* one another's emotional tides, not just past each other.

Research backs up what our souls instinctively know: communication matters. Couples who engage in more **positive and effective communication** report higher levels of relationship satisfaction and fewer negative cycles, while frequent negative communication is reliably linked with lower satisfaction. Other research shows that couples who spend more time interacting, especially when they talk *about their thoughts and feelings,* experience greater closeness and report more positive perceptions of one another. In short, check-ins aren't fluffy extras; they are evidence-backed practices that strengthen connection, lower conflict, and reduce emotional isolation.

But what *is* a check-in? It's not grilling your spouse like an investigative journalist after a long day — *"So... how **were** you feeling at 3:17 this afternoon?"* — although I've heard that negotiation is not out of the question for some couples! Instead, a check-in is a **safe space to share emotional updates;** what lifted your heart, what weighed on you, and where you need support. Gottman calls this kind of moment paying attention to "bids for connection" — the everyday invitations your spouse offers when they say or do something that opens the door for care, affirmation, or closeness. Our failure to respond to these bids is one of the subtle ways the connection dries up over time.

Emotional updates matter because unspoken feelings do not stay hidden; they leak into actions, tone, distance, and even the TV remote wars (which might actually not be about the remote at all). A daily check-in creates a rhythm where small things are no longer left to become big resentments. Research indicates that addressing minor emotional undercurrents early prevents them from turning into major conflicts later. These updates are not counseling sessions, problem-solving marathons, or debate forums, they are the practice of **intentional vulnerability** in the everyday now.

Check-ins also build emotional safety. When couples know they will have regular moments to share inner life without fear of judgment or automatic fixing, it cultivates trust. *"Be quick to hear, slow to speak, slow to anger,"* James writes, and that describes the posture of a good check-in: listening before defending, hearing before advising. James 1:19 is not a suggestion for Bible study; it's a relational blueprint for spouses. When your heart is genuinely heard, your wounds begin to heal, your joys are multiplied, and your unity deepens.

There's also a spiritual component that transcends psychology: check-ins provide a natural rhythm for **prayer together**. When spouses share their emotional state, they invite God into their inner world — fears, hopes, pains, and praises — rather than holding everything privately. Galatians 6:2 calls us to *"bear one another's burdens."* That bearing becomes nearly impossible if we never check in with one another in the first place.

Check-ins can feel awkward at first. You might worry about saying the wrong thing or stirring up old tensions. But growth often feels awkward before it feels normal. Remember the words of Scripture that remind us *"God's mercies are new every morning"*

(Lamentations 3:22–23). Similarly, every check-in is a *new opportunity* to be present and to grow in emotional intimacy. Over time, these intentional pauses become habits that strengthen friendship, deepen trust, and reinforce the sense that you and your spouse are *a team*, not coexisting, but co-journeying.

So, the next time you sit across from your spouse and feel like you're about to dive into surface logistics again, pause. Hold hands. Ask, *"What's something going on in your heart today?"* It might feel funny at first, but it will save you headaches later, and more importantly, keep your marriage from becoming a quiet ship drifting in parallel waters. Check-ins with emotional updates are not just communication tools, they are *habits of the heart* that honor God's design for connection, presence, and genuine love.

Setting Boundaries for Communication

One of the great myths of modern marriage is that access equals connection. We live in a world where we can reach each other instantly, texting from opposite sides of the couch, emailing from the same house, and scrolling while sitting inches apart. Yet many couples feel more disconnected than ever. The issue is not a lack of communication, but a lack of *protected* communication. Without boundaries, conversation becomes fragmented, distracted, and shallow. Proverbs 4:23 reminds us, *"Above all else, guard your heart, for everything you do flows from it."* In marriage, guarding the heart often begins by guarding the space where communication happens.

Boundaries are not walls meant to shut a spouse out; they are fences designed to protect what is valuable. When communication has no limits, everything competes for attention, phones, work emails, stress, notifications, and endless noise. Research consistently shows that digital distraction harms relational quality. Studies from the University of Texas found that the mere presence of a smartphone, even when not in use, reduces empathy and the depth of conversations. In other words, your phone doesn't even have to buzz to interrupt connection; it just has to exist. That's sobering... and also explains why so many serious conversations die somewhere between *"Hold on, let me respond to this real quick"* and complete emotional shutdown.

Setting **phone boundaries** is often the most immediate and impactful step couples can take. When phones dominate shared spaces, spouses unintentionally communicate, *"Something else has higher priority than you."* Establishing phone-free zones such as the dinner table, the bedroom, or during intentional check-ins, creates space for presence. Romans 12:10 calls us to *"outdo one another in showing honor,"* and few things communicate honor more clearly than undivided attention. No one expects perfection, but intentionality matters. Your spouse shouldn't have to compete with a glowing rectangle for eye contact.

Work boundaries are another critical area where communication often breaks down. Work stress doesn't stay neatly at the office; it follows us home, sits on the couch, and occasionally climbs into bed with us. While sharing about work is healthy, allowing work to dominate emotional energy is not. Studies on work-family spillover consistently show that unresolved job stress increases marital tension and emotional withdrawal. Scripture reminds us that there is *"a time for every purpose under heaven"* (Ecclesiastes 3:1). Healthy marriages recognize the importance of transitioning, intentionally shifting from work mode to spouse mode. Simple rituals, like a brief pause before entering the home or a few minutes of decompression before heavy conversation, can prevent stress from hijacking connection.

Another necessary boundary involves **stress sharing versus emotional dumping**. Marriage is a place of support, not emotional overflow without responsibility. Galatians 6 gives us a helpful balance: *"Carry each other's burdens"* (v.2) and *"each one should carry their own load"* (v.5). Healthy communication recognizes that your spouse is not your therapist, pressure valve, or emotional landfill. Boundaries help couples ask important questions before unloading: *Is now a good time? Are you in the emotional space to hear this?* This simple awareness preserves emotional safety and mutual respect.

Timing also matters. Many conflicts escalate not because the issue is severe, but because the moment is poorly chosen. Attempting deep conversations when one spouse is exhausted, hungry, or emotionally flooded rarely ends well. Proverbs 15:23 tells us, *"A word spoken at the right time ... how good it is!"* Setting boundaries around *when* serious conversations happen allows couples to talk with clarity instead of reactivity. Agreeing that either spouse can pause a conversation and revisit it later is not avoidance; it is wisdom.

Boundaries also protect **how** couples speak to one another. Emotional safety requires agreed-upon limits: no yelling, no name-calling, no sarcasm disguised as humor, and no weaponizing past failures. Ephesians 4:29 gives a clear standard, speech that builds up and gives

grace to the hearer. When couples establish these guardrails together, communication becomes a place of refuge rather than a source of fear. Boundaries don't silence honesty; they shape it so truth can be spoken without tearing down trust.

Some couples resist boundaries because they fear that restriction will limit intimacy. In reality, the opposite is true. Boundaries reduce resentment, increase emotional availability, and create room for vulnerability. Research from the Gottman Institute consistently shows that couples who protect time, attention, and emotional safety experience higher relationship satisfaction and stability. Boundaries don't weaken connection; they strengthen it by removing unnecessary competition for the heart.

It's important to note that boundaries work best when they are **agreed upon**, not imposed. Marriage thrives on partnership, not control. Boundaries should be revisited as seasons change such as new jobs, children, stressors, and responsibilities may require adjustments. And when boundaries are broken (because they will be), grace matters. Lamentations 3:22–23 reminds us that *"God's mercies are new every morning"*, and that same mercy should shape how couples grow together.

Setting boundaries for communication is an act of stewardship. It says, *"What we share here is sacred, and we are going to protect it."* In a world full of noise, intentional limits make room for love to be heard clearly. When communication is guarded with wisdom, marriage becomes not just functional, but deeply connected, rooted in presence, peace, and purpose.

> **Boundaries are not walls meant to shut a spouse out; they are fences designed to protect what is valuable**

How to Maintain Healthy Dialogue During Busy or Stressful Seasons

Every marriage eventually enters a season where life feels louder than love. Work deadlines pile up, kids need more than you have to give, finances tighten, health scares surface, or ministry demands stretch you thin. During these seasons, couples often assume that strained communication means something is wrong with the marriage itself. In reality, what's usually happening is far simpler, and far more human. Stress reduces capacity. Ecclesiastes reminds us that *"there is a season for everything"* (Eccl. 3:1), and that includes seasons when communication must adapt rather than disappear.

Stress doesn't just change schedules; it changes how the brain processes emotion. Research in relational psychology consistently shows that high stress lowers patience, reduces empathy, and increases the likelihood of misinterpreting tone. In other words, when life is heavy, your spouse's neutral comment can suddenly sound like criticism, and your response may come out sharper than intended. This is why many arguments during stressful seasons aren't really about the issue at hand. They're about two tired people trying to connect with depleted emotional reserves. Understanding this reframes conflict from *"You're the problem"* to *"We're under pressure."*

Healthy dialogue during busy seasons begins by **lowering expectations without lowering connection**. Couples often fall into all-or-nothing thinking: *If we can't talk deeply, why talk at all?* But Scripture invites a different perspective. *"Do not despise these small beginnings"* (Zech. 4:10). Five intentional minutes of connection can sustain intimacy when an hour-long conversation isn't possible. Faithfulness in small moments matters more than intensity in rare ones. This shift removes guilt and replaces it with grace.

One of the most important adjustments during stressful seasons is moving from **problem-solving to presence**. Stress triggers a fixing instinct, especially when one spouse wants to help, and the other wants to be heard. Yet many problems don't need immediate solutions; they need companionship. The book of Job offers a surprisingly practical lesson here: Job's friends were most helpful when they sat quietly with him. Their problems started when they opened their mouths. Sometimes the holiest response is, *"That sounds really heavy. I'm with you."* Presence lowers emotional temperature and keeps dialogue safe.

Busy seasons call for **micro-moments of connection**. These are brief but intentional points of contact that remind your spouse, *We're still in this together.* A short prayer before bed, a one-sentence emotional update, a hug that lasts a few seconds longer than usual, or a text that says, *"Thinking about you today"*, can carry enormous weight. Studies on relationship satisfaction consistently show that couples who maintain frequent, positive interactions, even brief ones, report greater closeness than couples who rely only on occasional "deep talks." Connection is cumulative.

Protecting **tone and words** becomes especially important when stress is high. Fatigue shortens patience, and under pressure, tone often communicates more than content. Proverbs 15:1 tells us, *"A gentle answer turns away wrath, but a harsh word stirs up anger."* Gentleness doesn't mean avoiding honesty; it means delivering truth with care. Sometimes love sounds like pausing before responding or choosing silence until emotions settle. This is not weakness; it is wisdom.

Equally important is knowing **when to pause conversations**. Not every issue needs immediate resolution, especially when one or both spouses are emotionally flooded. Healthy couples learn to say, *"This matters, but now isn't the best time. Let's come back to it."* Proverbs 19:11 reminds us that it brings honor to overlook an offense. Pausing is not avoidance when there is agreement to return, it's stewardship of emotional safety.

When words are limited, **prayer becomes a powerful form of dialogue**. Busy seasons often leave couples too tired to articulate everything they're feeling. Scripture reassures us that *"the Spirit helps us in our weakness... when we do not know what to pray for"* (Rom. 8:26). Even short, imperfect prayers invite God into the stress and realign hearts toward grace. Couples who pray together, even briefly, report greater emotional connection and resilience during difficult seasons.

It's also important to **revisit communication after the season**. Survival mode is sometimes necessary, but it should never become permanent. When the margin returns, couples should reflect together: What was hard? Where did we miss each other? What helped us stay connected? This reflection repairs any quiet distance that may have formed and restores fuller rhythms of communication. Scripture promises renewal for the weary (Isa. 40:31), and that renewal often begins with honest conversation.

Busy or stressful seasons do not define a marriage; they reveal it. How couples speak, listen, and show grace under pressure matters more than how long the pressure lasts. Healthy dialogue is not about saying everything perfectly, it's about choosing connection when it would be easier to withdraw. When couples meet stress with intentional presence, gentle words, and shared faith, marriage doesn't just survive busy seasons — it grows stronger through them.

Using Shared Hobbies and Spiritual Practices to Stimulate Communication Naturally

For many couples, communication feels hardest when it's forced. Sitting across from each other on the couch, staring eye to eye, waiting for meaningful words to appear, can feel less like a connection and more like a job interview. Ironically, some of the best conversations in marriage don't happen face-to-face at all. They happen side-by-side while walking, cooking, driving, serving, laughing, or praying together. God often meets us in motion, not just in moments of stillness, and shared activities create an environment where conversation can emerge naturally rather than under pressure.

There is something powerful about doing life *together*. Shared experiences reduce the emotional intensity that sometimes shuts conversation down. When attention is partially focused on an activity, defenses lower, expectations relax, and words come more freely. This is why couples often talk more openly on a walk than during a scheduled "serious talk." Scripture reflects this relational dynamic in a simple but exceptional way: *"Two are better than one, because they have a good return for their labor"* (Ecclesiastes 4:9). Shared effort doesn't just produce results, it produces connection.

Not all hobbies stimulate communication equally, however. Activities that encourage collaboration rather than competition tend to invite conversation rather than comparison. The goal isn't to find the most impressive or intense hobby; it's to find something that creates space for interaction. Whether it's cooking together, hiking, gardening, exercising, working on a project, or even tackling a shared goal, the activity becomes a bridge rather than a barrier. And yes, if your "shared hobby" involves assembling furniture, grace may need to increase exponentially in that moment!

Shared hobbies also reduce stress, which is one of the greatest enemies of healthy dialogue. Research consistently shows that couples who engage in leisure activities together report higher levels of marital satisfaction and emotional closeness. Enjoyment releases tension, laughter softens the heart, and joy makes it easier to talk. Proverbs 17:22 reminds us that *"a joyful heart is good medicine,"* and sometimes that medicine comes in the form of a shared moment that reminds you why you enjoy each other in the first place.

Alongside shared hobbies, **spiritual practices** serve as powerful anchors for communication. Prayer, Scripture reading, worship, and serving together create a shared spiritual language that deepens emotional understanding. Prayer, in particular, does something remarkable, it aligns hearts before it addresses issues. When couples pray together, they are reminded that they are on the same side, under the same authority, and dependent on the same grace. Jesus Himself promised, *"Where two or three gather in my name, there am I with them"* (Matthew 18:20). That promise applies just as much to the living room as it does to the church service.

Spiritual practices also create a uniquely safe space for emotional vulnerability. Praying for one another invites empathy. Expressing gratitude to God softens resentment. Reading Scripture together opens conversation around values, fears, hopes, and direction. As hearts grow closer to God, they often grow closer to each other. Ecclesiastes 4:12 reminds us that *"a cord of three strands is not quickly broken,"* and spiritual rhythms weave God into the daily fabric of marriage.

The key to sustaining shared hobbies and spiritual practices is **simplicity**. Many couples abandon good rhythms because they aim for idealized versions that don't fit real life. **A short prayer is better than no prayer.** A weekly walk is better than an annual retreat. Jesus invites the weary into rhythms that are light and life-giving, not burdensome (Matthew 11:28–30). Consistency matters more than complexity. Grace matters more than performance.

Shared practices should also invite conversation without demanding it. Silence can still be a connection. Not every moment needs to be filled with words. When couples remove the pressure to talk, communication often returns on its own. Trusting timing honors emotional safety and allows dialogue to unfold organically rather than being forced on a schedule.

As seasons of life change, shared rhythms will need to adapt. What worked before children, career changes, or health challenges may not work forever. But God is faithful to create new pathways of connection. *"See, I am doing a new thing!"* the Lord declares (Isaiah 43:19). Couples who revisit and adjust their shared practices stay flexible, resilient, and united.

Shared hobbies and spiritual practices remind couples that communication doesn't only happen through intentional conversations, it happens through intentional *togetherness*. When couples walk, serve, pray, and enjoy life side by side, communication becomes a natural overflow rather than a forced effort. Marriage grows not just through talking about life, but through living it together.

Healthy communication in marriage is not about saying everything perfectly or talking constantly, it's about creating rhythms that make connection normal rather than rare. Throughout this chapter, we've seen that communication thrives when it is intentional, protected, and woven into the everyday patterns of life. Daily check-ins, weekly alignment, monthly vision, healthy boundaries, grace during stressful seasons, and shared practices all work together to create a steady relational heartbeat.

A communication rhythm transforms marriage from reactive to relational. It removes pressure to *"fix everything now"* and replaces it with consistent presence, emotional safety, and spiritual alignment. Over time, these rhythms build trust, deepen intimacy, and create space for God to work in both hearts. Scripture reminds us that *"plans succeed with counsel"* (Proverbs 20:18), and a marriage that communicates well is one that plans, listens, and grows together with wisdom.

Communication is not just a skill to master; it is a stewardship to honor. When couples commit to creating rhythms that protect connection, marriage becomes a place where love is renewed, burdens are shared, and God's design is lived out daily. Healthy communication doesn't happen by accident; it happens when two people choose, again and again, to walk in step with each other and with God.

Chapter Twelve

Speaking, Listening, and Loving for Life

Biblical Foundation: Philippians 1:6, 1 Peter 4:8

Marriage doesn't come with a user manual unless you count the mysterious one written in invisible ink that only seems to appear *after* you mess something up. Most couples enter marriage believing they already know how to talk and listen. After all, you've been communicating your whole life. How hard can it be? Then one day you realize you've been having two entirely different conversations at the same time, both of you fluent, both of you sincere, and somehow still completely missing each other. Welcome to marriage communication, where tone matters more than vocabulary and silence can be louder than words.

The truth is, speaking, listening, and loving well in marriage are not skills you master once and then check off the list. It's a lifelong journey, one with detours, construction zones, and the occasional emotional pothole you swear *"came out of nowhere."* You'll have seasons where conversation flows easily and seasons where asking, *"How was your day?"* feels like opening negotiations at a high-stakes summit. Learning to communicate well isn't about winning arguments or having the perfect comeback; it's about growing in understanding, patience, and humility over time.

Listening, in particular, tends to stretch us more than speaking. Most of us listen just long enough to reload our response, not actually to understand. We nod, we smile, and internally we're already preparing our rebuttal like a closing argument. But real listening, the kind that says, "I care more about *you* than being right", requires slowing down, laying down our defenses, and sometimes admitting we missed the point entirely.

And then there's loving well because communication in marriage isn't just about words; it's about posture. **How we speak reveals what we value. How we listen reveals what we honor**. Loving well means choosing kindness when sarcasm feels easier, grace when frustration feels justified, and curiosity when assumptions want to take over. It means remembering that the person across from you is not the enemy, even when they forgot to replace the toilet paper roll *again*.

This chapter invites you into the reality that strong communication isn't built through perfection but through persistence. You won't always say the right thing. You won't always hear what your spouse meant. But with intentional effort, humility, and a whole lot of grace, you can learn to speak with clarity, listen with compassion, and love with depth over a lifetime. In marriage, communication isn't just about being heard; it's about being known and choosing to love each other well in every season of the journey.

How Communication Evolves Over the Years

Most couples enter marriage believing communication is primarily about learning what to say. Over time, they discover it is far more about learning how to listen, how to respond, and how to grow together. Communication in marriage is not fixed. It matures, stretches, breaks down, rebuilds, and deepens as the couple itself changes. Healthy marriages are not marked by perfect communication early on, but by a shared commitment to grow in understanding over the years.

Michelle and I have learned this firsthand. What worked for us in the early years doesn't always work now, and what works now would not have worked then. Communication evolves because people evolve.

Early marriage often feels like learning a new language spoken by someone who uses familiar words in unfamiliar ways. Couples are discovering how their spouse thinks, feels, processes emotion, and responds under stress. Even though you speak the same language, you quickly realize you don't always mean the same thing. The same sentence can land very differently depending on tone, timing, or fatigue level.

In those early years, communication is filled with moments like:

- Misunderstandings that require clarification

- Emotional reactions that reveal deeper expectations

- Realizations that "fine" rarely means what you thought it meant

Michelle and I weren't trying to miscommunicate, we were learning each other. That season required patience, curiosity, and humility. Growth happened when we learned to ask better questions rather than make quick assumptions.

As time passes, communication shifts from individual conversations to established patterns. Couples begin to anticipate responses, finish sentences, and assume intent based on history rather than the moment at hand. Familiarity can be a gift, but it can also quietly replace listening. The danger in long-term marriage isn't ignorance; it's assumption.

Michelle and I have caught ourselves responding to what we *thought* the other meant rather than what was actually being said. Healthy communication at this stage requires slowing down enough to listen again, even when you're confident you already know the answer.

Life seasons also reshape communication. Careers, ministry, children, stress, fatigue, finances, and responsibilities all affect how couples talk. In busy seasons, conversation often becomes practical and transactional. Many couples find that most of their communication revolves around logistics rather than connection:

- Schedules

- Responsibilities

- Problem-solving

There were seasons when Michelle and I realized our conversations had become efficient but not always intimate. That didn't mean love was gone; it meant life was loud. Mature couples learn to protect meaningful conversation intentionally, even when life feels overwhelming.

Conflict communication evolves as well. Early disagreements often feel emotional and reactive. Over time, healthy couples learn that maturity doesn't eliminate conflict — it transforms it. Growth shows up when couples learn to fight less defensively and listen more carefully. Michelle and I didn't stop disagreeing as we grew; we simply stopped trying to win. We learned that being right is far less important than being unified.

Over the years, spouses also learn whether it is emotionally safe to be honest. Every response trains the relationship toward either openness or withdrawal. When vulnerability is met with grace, communication deepens. When it's met with criticism or dismissal, silence slowly replaces honesty. Emotional safety is built when truth is handled gently, and tone matches intention. We've learned that how something is said often matters as much as what is said.

Long-term couples also develop strong non-verbal communication. Looks, pauses, sighs, and silence begin to speak volumes. This can be a gift, but it can also create misunderstanding when assumptions replace clarity. Just because you *can* read your spouse doesn't mean you always should. Healthy communication still asks questions rather than relying solely on interpretation.

As the years pass, couples become more aware of each other's weaknesses and their own. Mature communication becomes rooted in grace rather than perfection. Long-term marriages are sustained not because spouses stop failing, but because they stop keeping score. Michelle and I are both still growing, and grace has become the foundation that allows honest communication to continue.

Later seasons of marriage often require couples to rediscover conversation. When children leave home, or schedules slow down, couples may realize how much their communication has changed. This season can feel awkward or deeply rewarding, depending on whether communication has been nurtured along the way. The good news is that it is never too late to rebuild a connection through intentional conversation.

Communication in marriage reflects spiritual growth. As couples grow in Christ, their conversations should increasingly reflect humility, patience, gentleness, and self-control. Marriage becomes a living classroom of sanctification, where everyday conversations reveal how deeply the gospel has shaped the heart.

The goal of communication is not perfection; it is understanding. Flawless conversations do not define healthy marriages; rather, they are defined by a shared commitment to keep listening, keep growing, and keep choosing connection. Communication evolves because love matures. And when couples embrace that truth, they stop fearing change and start growing together.

Staying Teachable and Humble as You Grow Together

Staying teachable and humble in marriage is easy to value early on and surprisingly difficult to maintain over time. Most couples begin marriage open, curious, and willing to learn. Somewhere along the way, familiarity, confidence, and routine can quietly replace humility. Growth doesn't usually derail marriage — *unteachability* does.

Michelle and I didn't wake up one day deciding we had nothing left to learn. It happened gradually, in subtle ways. We began finishing each other's sentences, assuming motives, and thinking experience automatically meant understanding. Time together can build wisdom, but it can also build blind spots if humility isn't intentionally protected.

Humility in marriage is not a personality trait; it's a daily decision. Staying teachable means choosing openness over defensiveness, curiosity over assumption, and learning over proving a point. It's the willingness to admit, *"I might not see this clearly yet."* The longer couples are married, the easier it becomes to believe they already know what the other person is thinking. That belief rarely ends well.

Familiarity can quietly dull a teachable heart. When you've been together long enough, you stop asking questions and start relying on patterns. Michelle and I have had moments where we responded not to what the other was actually saying, but to what we expected them to say. We weren't listening, we were predicting. Humility slows the conversation down enough to hear what's actually being expressed in the moment, not what was said years ago.

Growth has a way of exposing blind spots you didn't know you had. New seasons bring new pressures, new responsibilities, and new versions of both spouses. What worked in one season may not work in the next. Teachable couples don't resist that reality; they adapt to it. Michelle has helped me see areas where I was confident but not always correct, and I've learned that correction is not rejection, it's an invitation to grow.

One of the quickest ways humility erodes in marriage is when being right becomes more important than being united. Winning an argument feels good for about ten minutes; preserving unity lasts far longer. Michelle and I have learned that if the goal of a conversation is to win, we've already lost. Teachable hearts ask, *"What can I learn here?"* instead of *"How do I defend myself?"*

Staying teachable requires emotional safety. No one remains open to growth in an environment where mistakes are punished or weaknesses are mocked. Humility thrives where grace lives. Michelle and I have had to learn how to give feedback without using it as a weapon. Growth happens when honesty is welcomed, and correction is wrapped in love, not sarcasm.

Apologies reveal humility more clearly than almost anything else. Early in marriage, apologies can feel heavy and awkward. Over time, healthy couples learn to apologize more quickly, more clearly, and with fewer explanations. Michelle and I still laugh about how long we used to circle an apology before actually saying the words. Humility shortens that distance. Owning mistakes doesn't weaken a marriage, it strengthens trust.

Teachable couples also recognize they don't have to figure everything out alone. Humility invites outside wisdom including scripture, mentors, counselors, books, and trusted voices. There is strength in learning from those who have walked ahead. Marriage becomes dangerous when couples isolate themselves and assume no one else has anything to teach them.

Spiritual growth should deepen humility, not inflate confidence. As couples grow in Christ, they should become quicker to listen, slower to react, and more generous with grace. Michelle and I have found that when our hearts are soft toward God, they're usually softer toward each other as well. Spiritual pride erodes teachability, but spiritual maturity produces gentleness and patience.

Marriage also requires humility because change is inevitable. Both spouses will grow, shift, and surprise each other. Teachable couples don't cling to who their spouse used to be; they learn to love who they are becoming. Michelle and I are not the same people we were when we said, "I do," and that's not a threat — it's a gift. Humility allows couples to grow without growing apart.

The goal of staying teachable is not perfection; it's progress together. Humble marriages remain curious, flexible, and open because they value growth more than ego. Staying teachable means choosing to grow side by side rather than competing for who is right.

Marriage thrives when both spouses remain students of God, of each other, and of the journey they're walking together. When couples protect humility, they protect their ability to grow. And when they grow together, they don't just stay married, they become stronger, wiser, and more deeply connected along the way.

Choosing Forgiveness and Grace Daily

Choosing forgiveness and grace daily sounds noble in theory and exhausting in practice. Most couples don't struggle with the *idea* of forgiveness; they struggle with its frequency. Marriage has a way of revealing just how often grace is needed, not only for big wounds, but for small irritations, careless words, unmet expectations, and moments when love feels more like work than romance. Healthy marriages are not those where offense never occurs, but those where forgiveness is practiced consistently.

Michelle and I learned early on that forgiveness in marriage is rarely a one-time event. It is far more often a daily decision. Some days it's about forgiving something significant, and other days it's about forgiving tone, timing, or tension. Scripture reminds us to *"bear with one another and forgive one another... as the Lord has forgiven you"* (Colossians 3:13). That command assumes there will be something to forgive — and often.

Grace is usually necessary when expectations fall short. Many of the frustrations couples experience aren't caused by intentional harm, but by unspoken assumptions. We expect our spouse to know what we need, how we feel, or why something matters to us.

When those expectations go unmet, offense quietly takes root. Michelle and I have had moments where the real issue wasn't what happened, but what one of us expected *not* to happen. Grace begins when we release the demand that our spouse always gets it right.

Forgiveness becomes even more critical because resentment rarely announces itself loudly. It grows quietly. When forgiveness is delayed, small offenses pile up and begin shaping how spouses interpret each other's words and actions. Hebrews 12:15 warns that bitterness can take root and defile many. Daily forgiveness uproots resentment before it hardens into something far more damaging.

Forgiveness does not mean pretending hurt never happened, nor does it excuse sin or dismiss responsibility. Jesus modeled this perfectly. When He forgave, He did not deny truth, He addressed it with grace. He extended forgiveness while still calling people to repentance and transformation. In marriage, forgiveness protects unity without minimizing honesty. It creates space for healing instead of punishment.

Grace also changes the tone of communication. When forgiveness is present, conversations soften. Defensiveness decreases, listening increases, and empathy replaces accusation. Michelle and I have noticed that when we approach conversations with grace, we're far more likely to resolve issues quickly. When grace is absent, even small discussions can feel heavy and exhausting. Proverbs 15:1 reminds us that a gentle answer turns away wrath, and grace gives that gentleness room to grow.

One of the hardest parts of forgiveness is letting go of the desire for repayment. Unforgiveness often keeps score; who hurt who, how often, and how badly. Grace tears up the scoreboard. Jesus addressed this directly when Peter asked how many times he should forgive, and Jesus responded, *"seventy-seven times"* (Matthew 18:21–22). His point wasn't math; it was posture. Forgiveness in marriage means choosing restoration over repayment.

Christian marriage draws its deepest understanding of forgiveness from the gospel itself. We forgive because we have been forgiven much. Jesus' life was marked by radical grace toward sinners, critics, betrayers, and even those who crucified Him. On the cross, He prayed, *"Father, forgive them"* (Luke 23:34). Remembering how freely grace has been given to us changes how tightly we cling to offenses against us.

Apologies and forgiveness must work together for grace to thrive. **Forgiveness does not eliminate the need for repentance, and repentance does not eliminate the need for forgiveness.** Michelle and I have learned that sincere apologies, without excuses or explanations, open the door for real healing. And forgiving quickly doesn't mean healing instantly. Some wounds take time, and grace remains patient while trust is rebuilt.

Jesus never rushed people through healing, but He also never withheld grace until they were fully restored. He met people where they were and walked with them forward. That same posture is essential in marriage. Grace stays present even after forgiveness is spoken.

Over time, daily forgiveness sustains long-term love. Long marriages survive not because spouses stop hurting each other, but because they stop holding grudges against each other. Grace keeps hearts soft, conversations honest, and love resilient. Michelle and I are still learning this. Some days, grace flows easily; other days, it feels more like obedience than emotion. But every time we choose forgiveness, we choose connection.

Marriage is not a place where perfect people meet, it's a place where forgiven people learn how to forgive again and again. When couples choose grace daily, they don't erase conflict, but they redeem it. And in doing so, they reflect the heart of Christ in one of the most visible relationships God has designed.

Celebrating Progress Rather than Perfection

Many couples enter marriage with an unspoken expectation that, with enough time and effort, they, or their spouse, will eventually arrive at some polished, fully formed version of themselves. The problem is that perfection is a destination marriage was never meant to reach. Growth, on the other hand, is the goal God designed. When couples chase perfection, they often grow discouraged. When they learn to celebrate progress, they find joy, freedom, and momentum.

Michelle and I have learned that marriage doesn't progress in giant leaps nearly as often as we hoped. Most growth shows up quietly in better reactions, shorter arguments, quicker apologies, and increased awareness. Early on, we were tempted to focus on what still needed fixing. Over time, we realized that constantly pointing out gaps actually slowed growth rather than accelerating it.

Perfection creates pressure, and pressure rarely produces lasting change. When perfection becomes the standard, effort feels invisible, and progress feels insufficient. Spouses can begin to think, *"Why try if it's never enough?"* Celebrating progress shifts the atmosphere. It communicates, *"I see you trying, and it matters."* That kind of encouragement builds confidence and invites continued growth.

Scripture consistently shows us that God works through process, not instant results. Sanctification is gradual. Philippians 1:6 reminds us that *"God is faithful to complete the work He began"*, not all at once, but over time. When couples expect instant transformation, they often grow impatient with each other. When they align their expectations with God's process, patience and grace increase.

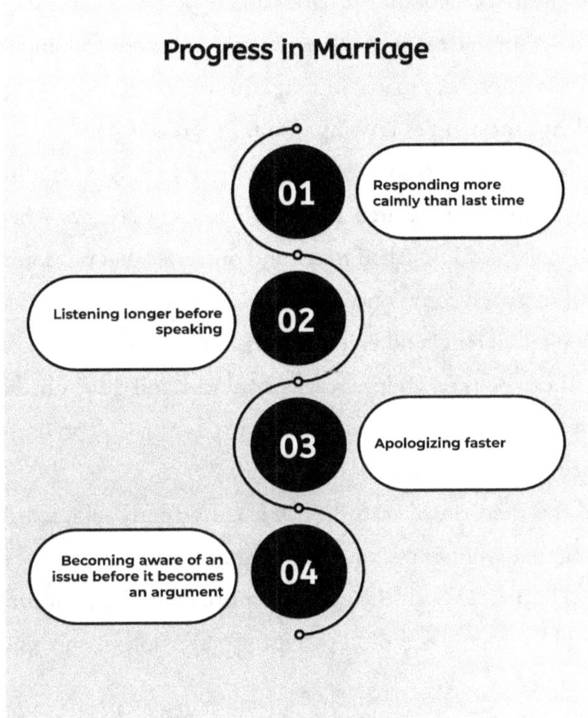

Some of the most meaningful changes in marriage are also the smallest. Progress often looks like:

- Responding more calmly than last time

- Listening longer before speaking

- Apologizing faster

- Becoming aware of an issue before it becomes an argument

Michelle and I have learned to celebrate those moments, even when they don't feel dramatic. Growth rarely announces itself with fireworks; most of the time, it shows up quietly and consistently.

Criticism tends to focus on what's missing, while celebration highlights what's improving. When correction outweighs affirmation, spouses brace themselves rather than opening their hearts. Celebrating progress doesn't ignore areas that still need growth, it simply refuses to let those areas overshadow what God is already doing. Encouragement fuels change far more effectively than constant critique.

Another challenge for couples is comparison. Progress is personal, not competitive. Measuring your marriage against someone else's filtered highlight reel distorts reality and steals joy. Growth should be measured against where you were, not where someone else appears to be. Michelle and I have had to remind ourselves that our journey is ours, and God's work in our marriage doesn't need to look like anyone else's.

Progress also looks different in different seasons. Some seasons bring visible growth and breakthroughs; others focus on endurance, faithfulness, and quiet obedience. Not every season feels productive, but every season can be purposeful. Celebrating progress means recognizing faithfulness even when results feel slow.

Jesus modeled this perspective beautifully. He consistently acknowledged small steps of faith. He celebrated willingness, obedience, and direction, even when people were far from perfect. He praised faith the size of a mustard seed and affirmed effort when outcomes were still forming. Jesus didn't wait for perfection to encourage growth, and neither should couples.

When progress is celebrated, grace increases and pride decreases. Couples become more patient with each other and more honest about where they still need help. Michelle and I have found that naming progress out loud softens our hearts and strengthens our partnership. It reminds us that we're growing *together*, not evaluating each other from opposite sides.

Celebrating progress keeps marriage focused on becoming more like Christ rather than becoming flawless. Marriage was never meant to be a performance — it's a process. When couples learn to honor growth rather than demand perfection, they create an environment where love can breathe, change can happen, and joy can return.

Marriage thrives not when spouses get everything right, but when they keep moving in the right direction together. And every step forward, no matter how small, is worth celebrating.

Leaving a Communication Legacy for Children and Others

Marriage is never lived in isolation. Whether couples realize it or not, the way they communicate is always being watched, learned from, and carried forward. Words spoken in the kitchen, tone used during conflict, silence after disagreement, and reconciliation after tension all preach a sermon. Long before children understand theology, they understand tone. Long before they learn relationship principles, they observe relationship patterns. Communication leaves a legacy.

Michelle and I have learned that our **children don't just hear what we say, they absorb how we say it.** They notice whether conversations are marked by patience or sarcasm, respect or defensiveness, grace or tension. They watch how we speak when we're tired, stressed, or frustrated. And perhaps most importantly, they watch how we recover when communication breaks down.

Marriage becomes the loudest classroom of communication in the home. What children see modeled between a husband and wife shapes how they will one day speak to friends, coworkers, spouses, and even God. A marriage marked by respect teaches respect. A marriage marked by harshness teaches fear. A marriage marked by grace teaches grace. Children don't need perfect examples; they need *honest ones*.

One of the greatest misconceptions parents carry is that conflict itself damages children. In reality, unresolved or unhealthy conflict does. Children benefit from seeing disagreement handled with humility, listening, and reconciliation. Michelle and I have had moments where conversations got tense, and little eyes were watching. What mattered most wasn't that we disagreed, it was that they later saw us apologize, soften, forgive, and reconnect. That taught far more than pretending everything was fine ever could.

Tone is one of the most powerful teachers in the home. Children quickly learn whether it is safe to speak honestly by observing how parents speak to each other. If tone is harsh, dismissive, or explosive, kids learn to withhold. If tone is respectful, calm, and patient, even during disagreement, kids learn that honesty is welcomed. Michelle and I have learned that sometimes the greatest lesson we teach our kids is how we lower our voices when emotions rise.

Apologies are another cornerstone of a communication legacy. When parents apologize, to each other and to their children, they demonstrate strength, not weakness. Children who see adults own mistakes grow up understanding repentance, accountability, and humility. Michelle and I still laugh at how uncomfortable apologies felt early on, especially when kids were watching. But over time, we realized that saying "I was wrong" out loud was shaping their hearts far more than saving face ever could.

Grace-filled communication also shapes how children understand God. A home where correction is paired with love, truth with patience, and discipline with restoration reflects the heart of the gospel. When grace is present in everyday conversations, children learn that failure isn't final and that love doesn't disappear when mistakes are made. How parents communicate often becomes the lens through which children interpret God's character.

Consistency matters deeply. Children are remarkably perceptive when words and actions don't match. A communication legacy is built not through one good conversation, but through repeated patterns over time. Michelle and I have learned that credibility isn't built in public moments, it's built in private ones, when no one is watching... except the kids who always are.

This legacy doesn't stop with children. Couples are also modeling communication for extended family, friends, church communities, and younger couples who are watching quietly. Healthy communication becomes a form of ministry without a platform. The way spouses listen, speak, and forgive often permits others to grow in their own relationships.

One of the most powerful lessons couples can pass on is how to repair after a breakdown. Children need to see that tension doesn't mean the relationship is over. They need to see conversations circle back, apologies offered, forgiveness extended, and unity restored. Redemption is learned by watching it lived out.

Leaving a communication legacy is not about perfection, it's about faithfulness. **Children don't need flawless parents; they need growing ones.** They need to see adults who are committed to learning, changing, and choosing to love again and again. The legacy that lasts is not *"we never fought,"* but *"we always found our way back to each other."*

Marriage was never meant to be lived only for the present moment. Every conversation, every conflict, every act of grace is shaping something beyond today. Couples are writing a story not only with their words, but with their tone, posture, and willingness to grow. That story will be remembered long after specific conversations are forgotten.

Michelle and I are still learning this. We don't always get it right, but we are committed to getting it *better*. And we've learned that when communication is handled with humility, grace, and intention, it becomes one of the most powerful gifts we can pass on to the next generation.

Marriage is a mission. It is a calling to reflect Christ's love not just to one another, but to everyone watching, especially the children sitting quietly nearby, learning what love sounds like. When couples commit to communicating with truth and grace, they don't just strengthen their marriage; they shape the future.

The legacy you leave won't be built on perfect words, but on faithful ones. And when couples choose to speak life, listen well, forgive freely, and grow humbly, they leave behind something far greater than memories, they leave a model worth following.

Resources

Chapter 1:

1. National Center for Family and Marriage Research. (2018). "Divorce Rates by Year." Retrieved from [https://www.bgsu.edu/ncfmr/resources/data-sets/divorce-rates.html]

2. Barna Group. (2016). "The State of the Church: Marital Satisfaction Among Christians." Retrieved from [https://www.barna.com/research/the-state-of-the-church-2016]

3. Lifeway Research. (2017). "The Importance of Communication in Marriage." Retrieved from [https://lifewayresearch.com/2017/04/12/importance-communication-marriage/]

4. American Psychological Association. (2018). "Understanding Couples and Marriage." Retrieved from [https://www.apa.org/topics/marriage]

5. Snyder, D. K., & Whisman, M. A. (2003). "The Emotional Impact of Divorce: A Family System Perspective." Family Relations. 52(2), 131-141.

Chapter 2:

1. American Psychological Association. Couples Who Listen Well Have Stronger Relationships.

2. American Association for Marriage and Family Therapy. The Importance of Effective Communication in Relationships.

3. Microsoft Corporation. (2015). Attention Spans: How Long is Too Long. Retrieved from [https://www.microsoft.com/en-us/research/wp-content/uploads/2016/05/AttentionSpansResearchReport.pdf]

4. University of Washington. Interruptions in Couples' Communication.

5. Buehler, C., & Gerard, J. (2002). The Role of Communication in Conflict Resolution in Marriage. Journal of Marriage and Family, 64(1), 156-170.

6. Cutrona, C. E., & Russell, D. W. (1990). Linking Social Support to Quality of Life. Journal of Marriage and Family, 52(2), 379–393.

7. Doss, B. D., & Murdock, N. L. (2004). Active Listening and the Couples' Sense of Connection. Personal Relationships, 11(2), 149-164.

Chapter 3:

1. Gottman, John M. "The Seven Principles for Making Marriage Work." Crown Publishers, 1999.

2. Gottman, John M., and Nan Silver. "The New Science of Love: How the Understanding of Marital Relationships Can Change Your Life." 3rd ed., Three Rivers Press, 2015.

3. Kessler, R. C., et al. "The Epidemiology of Major Depressive Disorder: Results from the National Comorbidity survey replication (NCS-R)." Journal of the American Medical Association, vol. 289, no. 23, 2003, pp. 3095-3105.

4. Amato, Paul R., and Bruce Keith. "Consequences of Parental Divorce for Adult Well-Being: Meta-Analysis." Psychological Bulletin, vol. 127, no. 5, 2001, pp. 748-795.

5. Lawrence, Ellen, et al. "The Impact of Critical Communication on the Mental Health of Couples." Journal of Marriage and Family, vol. 61, no. 2, 1999, pp. 456-465.

Chapter 4:

1. The Holy Bible, New International Version. (1984). Zondervan. (Genesis 1:27, 1 Corinthians 12:12-14).

2. Myers, I. B., & McCaulley, M. H. (1985). Manual: A Guide to the Development and Use of the Myers-Briggs Type Indicator. Consulting Psychologists Press.

3. American Psychological Association. (2020). "Marriage and divorce." Retrieved from [APA website](https://www.apa.org/topics/divorce).

4. Vazire, S., & Funder, D. C. (2006). "Beyond the Person-Situation Debate: The Role of Personality in the Context of Relationships." Journal of Personality, 74(6), 1077-1100. DOI: 10.1111/j.1467-6494.2006.00412.x.

5. Levenson, R. W., Carstensen, L. L., & Gottman, J. M. (1993). "The Influence of Social Environment on Emotion in Marriage." Emotion, 36(3), 621-631. DOI: 10.100 7/BF02159380.

Chapter 6:

1. Manalel, J. A., et al. (2019). *Beyond Destructive Conflict: Implications of Marital Tension for Marital Well-Being. National Center for Biotechnology Information (PMC).*

This longitudinal study examined how destructive conflict behaviors relate to lower marital satisfaction and well-being, extending conflict research beyond overt behaviors.

2. "Relationship of Conflict Resolution Styles in Marriage with Marital Adjustment and Satisfaction." (2022). *ResearchGate.* This review discusses how different conflict resolution styles (constructive vs. destructive) relate to marital happiness and adjustment.

3. "Role of Conflict Resolution Styles and Emotional Intelligence." *PJPR Scientific Journal.* This article explains classifications of conflict resolution strategies—constructive and destructive—and their implications on relationship quality.

4. Mandal, E. (2022). *Mindfulness, Relationship Quality, and Conflict Resolution. PMC.* This research found constructive conflict methods (dialogue, mutual listening) positively correlated with relationship quality, while destructive strategies were linked to lower satisfaction.

5. Gottman, J. (1999). *The Seven Principles for Making Marriage Work.* A foundational book outlining research-based principles for healthy marital interactions, including conflict patterns.

6. *The Mindful Marriage: Create Your Best Relationship Through Understanding and Managing Yourself* by Ron L. Deal, Nan Deal, Terry Hargrave, and Sharon Hargrave, published by Worthy Books in January 2025, ISBN 978-1546007388.

Chapter 7:

1. Gottman, J. M. & Levenson, R. W. — *Marital processes predictive of later dissolution: Behavior, physiology, and health* (Journal of Personality and Social Psychology, 1992).

Chapter 11:

1. Lavner, J. A., et al. *Does Couples' Communication Predict Marital Satisfaction, or Does Satisfaction Predict Positive Communication? Frontiers in Psychology,* National Institutes of Health.

2. Gottman, J. (multiple articles). *Improve Your Relationship by Paying Attention to "Bids"* and related blog pieces from *The Gottman Institute.*

3. Lavner, J. A., Karney, B. R., & Bradbury, T. N. *Within-Couple Associations Between Communication and Relationship Satisfaction. Frontiers in Psychology.*

About the author

Daniel Moore has called Neosho, Missouri home his whole life. He's been married to his wife, Michelle, for over 20 years, and together they've built a full and busy life with three (now adult) children, two of them which have awesome spouses, one dog, and now four granddaughters who keep them smiling. Daniel and Michelle host the podcast *Marriage Life and More*, where they share weekly conversations about God's design for marriage. Daniel also hosts *Connecting the Gap*, a Bible study podcast that helps listeners dig deeper into Scripture. When he's not working at a Christian radio station or running his computer business, you can usually find him out on a bike ride, kayaking, catching a football game, or just spending time with Michelle, the thing he enjoys most of all!

You Can Connect with us at:

https://www.marriagelifeandmore.com

https://www.connectingthegap.net

https://x.com/ctgaponline

https://www.facebook.com/ctgaponline/

https://www.instagram.com/ctgaponline/

Also Available

This book is a Christ-centered guide that redefines marriage not just as a relationship, but as a divine calling. Rooted in biblical truth, this book explores God's original intent for marriage and offers practical wisdom for couples seeking to grow in love, unity, and purpose. Through topics such as covenant commitment, spiritual intimacy, servant-hearted leadership, and shared ministry, readers are invited to see their marriage as a powerful expression of the gospel. Whether you're newlyweds or seasoned partners, this book will inspire you to embrace your marriage as a mission and experience deeper fulfillment through Christ.

This is available in paperback, hardback, and Kindle on Amazon.com. http://bit.ly/4n Ms7kP

The e-book is also available on Google Play Books and Apple Books.

This study guide is a companion to *Marriage as a Mission – Living Out God's Design for Marriage*, designed to help couples and small groups dive deeper into God's purpose for marriage. Each section offers thought-provoking questions, practical exercises, and biblical insights that guide husbands and wives toward a Christ-centered relationship. Whether used individually, as a couple, or in a group setting, this guide will help you apply God's Word to real-life situations and strengthen your marriage as a reflection of His love and mission in the world.

This study guide is available in paperback format on Amazon only. http://bit.ly/4nac67e

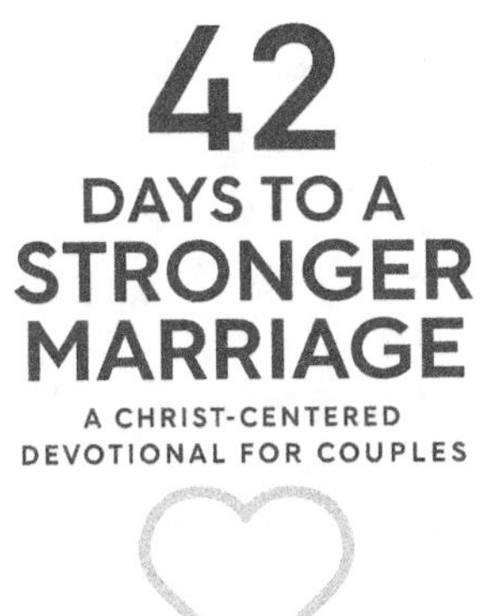

Strengthen your marriage in just 42 days with this **Christ-centered devotional for couples!** *42 Days to a Stronger Marriage* offers practical, biblical guidance to deepen **love, trust, and intimacy** in your relationship. Each day includes a Scripture (ESV), a thoughtful devotional, reflection questions, a couples' challenge, and a prayer, making it easy to apply God's Word to everyday life.

This is available in paperback, hardback, and Kindle on Amazon.com. http://bit.ly/4n Ms7kP

The e-book is also available on Google Play Books.